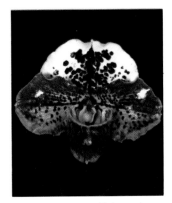

Paph. Erie

Anyone for orchids?

Paph. Ogallala 'Bronx' AM/AOS
Penn Valley Orchids

Paphiopedilum Maudiae 'Silverado' AM/AOS—81 pts
(Callosum × Lawrenceanum)
A good beginner plant

Anyone for orchids?

by Georgiana Webber

SCHIFFER LIMITED

Box E, Exton, PA 19341

ANYONE FOR ORCHIDS?

Anyone for Orchids?

Copyright © 1978, Schiffer Limited, Box E, Exton, Pa. 19341

Library of Congress catalog card number: 78-57571

ISBN 0-916838-15-3

Printed in the United States of America

To Carl, Sam and George

PREFACE

If you've tried growing everything from Aspidistras to Zinnias and you haven't tried Orchids, you don't know what you're missing. They are easier to grow than African Violets and far more posh than any other plant. The variety available boggles the mind (over 56,000 species and hybrids).

I must warn you, though, that ever since their introduction to England in the 19th Century they have caused an "orchid mania" that continues to this day.

My own first orchid was a Catasetum though I didn't know it. I bought it for $1.98 in a Sears store in Florida as a dormant back bulb. Back north in Philadelphia, it was placed on a gravel filled tray under fluorescent lights in a big bay window and, in due course, it bloomed. A trip to the library for some orchid books was quickly followed by the purchase of some more of these marvelous exotic orchids and the fever had struck.

This book, in a way, is a history of this fascination with orchids. It has led to great friendships, lots of reading, trips to exotic places (sometimes only through books) and the joy and frustration of growing the world's most fabulous plants.

Catesetum pileatum 'Riopelle' CCM/AOS—85 pts
Exhibited by Jim & Marie Riopelle
A collector's item

ANYONE FOR ORCHIDS?

The author wishes to thank the many people who have helped her and encouraged her in the preparation of this volume. Evelyn and Harold Walker have been of invaluable help in sharing their wide knowledge of orchids.

She wishes to thank Richard L. Seifert for his help in hybridizing. A special word of thanks is due to Dr. W. W. Wilson for much advice and his beautiful pictures. Richard L. Peterson, executive director of the American Orchid Society has been a great sounding board and generous beyond belief in lending pictures and materials for this volume.

She also wishes to thank her husband, Carl for his kind support and help with pictures and wiring diagrams. Special thanks are due to Bob Scully, Jr., of Jones and Scully, and to Robert R. Johnson of Rod McLellan Co.

Your AOS Bulletins give names of commercial sources for plants and supplies.

TABLE OF CONTENTS

INTRODUCTION

Why not orchids?

Plant lovers unite; you have nothing to lose but your Philodendron. For the price of a Cactus you can have a Cattleya. Even when out of bloom, Paphs are prettier than Porthos. Trade in your spider plant for a Stanhopea. Why not grow the best? Unless you go for the connoisseur plants priced from $100.00–$1,000.00 you can buy orchids for not much more than Swedish ivy. Little plants from a flask may run 50¢ a piece; seedlings $3.00–$10.00 or $12.00. Not every orchid looks like it belongs in a corsage. Here are some pictures of flowers of the most common orchids.

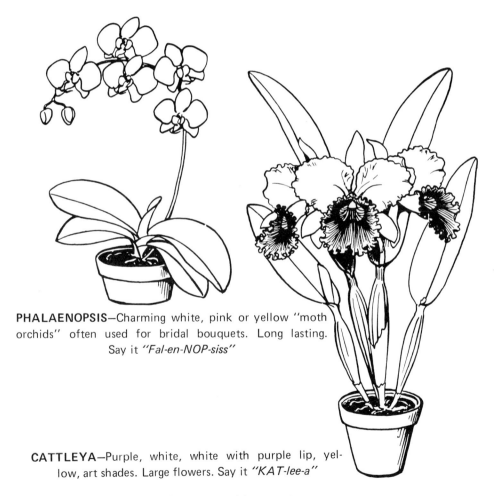

PHALAENOPSIS—Charming white, pink or yellow "moth orchids" often used for bridal bouquets. Long lasting. Say it *"Fal-en-NOP-siss"*

CATTLEYA—Purple, white, white with purple lip, yellow, art shades. Large flowers. Say it *"KAT-lee-a"*

11

ANYONE FOR ORCHIDS?

CYPRIPEDIUM—"Lady slippers" in pastel or exotic dark colors. Plants small and compact. Blooms long lasting. Say it *"Sip-ree-PEE-dee-um"*

Odontoglossum

Stanhopea

Cycnoches

Peristeria

Miltonia

Angraecum

ONCIDIUM—Little yellow or pink "dancing lady" flowers with dozens to a stem. Look for their ballet skirts. Say it *"On-SID-ee-um"*

(Sketches by Marion Ruff Sheehan)

12

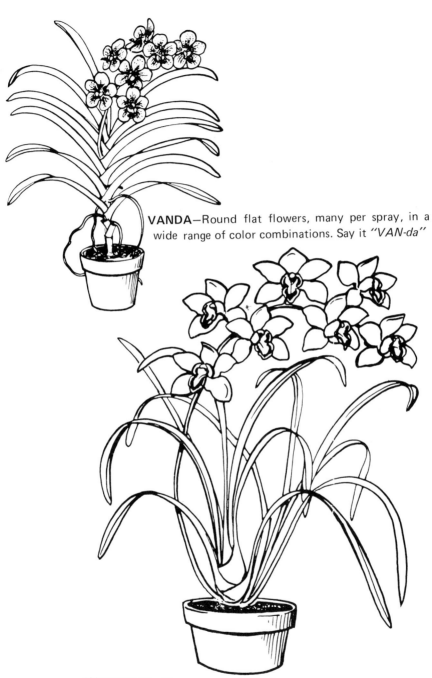

VANDA—Round flat flowers, many per spray, in a wide range of color combinations. Say it *"VAN-da"*

CYMBIDIUM—Flowers stay fresh 2 or 3 months. Lovely pastel colors on big spikes in spring. Used for corsages. *Say it "Sim-BID-ee-um"*

13

ANYONE FOR ORCHIDS?

WHAT IS AN ORCHID?

Now that you've seen those pretty pictures, I suppose I should tell you what an orchid is.

For those scientifically inclined, you can read this description written by a botanist. All others skip on to the next paragraph.

Perennial herbs with tuberous or fibrous roots, stems without annual rings, minute embryo with one cotyledon, leaves with parallel venation, flowers with three sepals and three alternating petals, one of which is modified into a lip; floral sexual organs united into a single structure called a column; pollen often united into waxy spherical masses called pollinia, ovary one chambered with three carpels, inferior, with abundant minute ovules.

Maybe, you'll never need all that, but if you do, there it is. Now, what is an orchid?

Orchids are members of the botanical family *Orchidaceae,* the largest family of flowering plants. Their flower structure makes them orchids. Vegetative growth and habit varies all over the lot, but all orchids have a column which is a fusion of the male (staminate) and female (pestillate) reproductive organs. All orchid flowers have three sepals and three petals although some may be reduced or fused. The lip or labellum, often the most conspicuous part of the flower, is a modified petal. The pollen of orchids is fused into 2–8 masses called pollinia and located under an anther cap on the column. Separated from the anther cap by the rostellum is the stigmatic surface, and below it the ovary. When fertilized the ovary turns into a seed pod containing about 1 million seeds. Orchids are monocots (a single seed leaf). They have parallel leaf veins and are related to lilies, bananas, palms and grasses.

Orchids fall roughly into two main groups according to their growth habit.

Sympodial orchids have roots rhizome stem or pseudobulb and leaves. They put on one growth at a time. Cattleyas are an example of sympodial growth habit.

Monopodial orchids have roots, a main stem that keeps getting longer and flower spikes, that grow from the leaf axils. Phalaenopsis and Vandas are examples of monopodial growth habit.

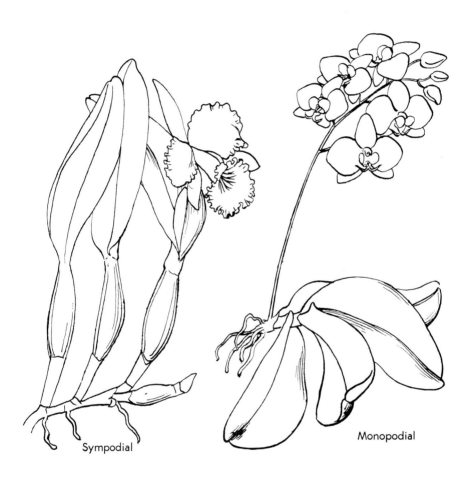

Sympodial

Monopodial

ANYONE FOR ORCHIDS?

Cymbidium Nila 'Green Gold'
Rod McLellan Co.

Phalaenopsis Iris Sea . . . serene elegance
Rod McLellan Co.

I

Growing Orchids
Without a Greenhouse

Window Sills

The lack of a greenhouse should not deter anyone. Almost any exposure, except due North or due West, is possible. North, of course, is too dark to make anything bloom, and West is too hot in the summer. Outdoor light can be supplemental with fluorescent strips or "plant grow" spots.

A big bay window is ideal, but any window can be turned into a mini-orchid area. First of all, you need gravel filled trays to catch the drips and add humidity. If the trays can be fitted with racks to keep the plants up off the gravel, so much the better. Orchids don't like "wet feet" and do like air circulation. Custom made copper trays are elegant, but plastic will do. White marble chips are attractive, but all stones will have to be washed in a Clorox solution and rinsed carefully whenever algae builds up. Another elegant solution is to use a plastic egg crate (easy to saw). It is used in the ceilings of modern offices.

A small "hi fi" fan to provide good air circulation is the next addition. You can buy this at Radio Shack or an equivalent shop.

A good mister, watering can, a Rain Bottle and a bulb baster to suck up excess water from the trays are needed. The Rain Bottle is a squeeze plastic bottle with a sprinkler top (from Design Research).

In an area so small, the grower must be very careful in plant selection. He will be told to try Paphiopedilums and Phalaenopsis. Some "Paphs," of course, will do quite well but "Phals" are so finicky about humidity and fresh air that they may drop their buds and sulk. And, after all, orchid growers want to grow "real" orchids, the cattleyas. Try a couple. Find a fall blooming white; they take less light, and fall bloomers can go outside for the summer and be brought in ready to bloom.

ANYONE FOR ORCHIDS?

Try some Paphs especially ones with mottled foliage. They will do better in house temperatures than the solid green leaved ones. Paphs, grown in the house, should be repotted once a year and do better with three to five growths. The mixes tend to break down rapidly in the house. If this happens, the roots will rot or be burned from over fertilization. Paphs are not big feeders, and must never be dried out.

A couple of other sure fire beginning plants are *Epidendrum cochleatum* which has octopus shaped flowers and blooms all fall and *Brassavola nodosa,* called "Lady of the Night," which is fragrant at night and not fussy. It will do well mounted on a plaque or cork.

Photo by John C. Kraurer, M

Epi cochleatum var. Sophia AM/AOS—84 pts
Exhibited by Mrs. Sophia Norman
Great beginner plant

Brassavola nodosa 'Eleanor' CCM/AOS—82 pt
Exhibited by John Herbert
Lady of the Night—everyone's favorite

ANYONE FOR ORCHIDS?

Miniature orchids are great for window growers. Any of the new hybrid equitant Oncidiums will shower you with tiny colorful blooms and not take up much room. Grow them on "rafts" or in pots. *Neofinetia falcata* has tiny white flowers with a long spur and will do well. Another good miniature is *Epidendrum polybulbon.* Try *Leptotes bicolor* and *unicolor.* The very small *Cattleya luteola* is an easy grower. Terrestrials that are grown for their jewel-like foliage like Haemaria may even bloom.

If you can summer your plants outside and have the room, expand your collection to include a fall blooming miniature Cymbidium that will be already in spike when brought into house just before frost. They must have the cool fall temperatures to bloom at all.

Leptotes bicolor var. 'Blue Crest' CCM/AOS—87 pts Exhibited by Edward J. Jank
One of the best of the miniatures

Stay away from Brassias (spikes too big), Oncidium sphace-latum (too weedy) Odontoglossums, Miltonias, Madsdevallias and Sophronitis (house temperatures too warm). Don't buy plants to grow on a window sill just because they are pretty. After you are successful try some of the plants listed on page 31 in the chapter on *Light Growing* or on page 42 in the chapter, *Your First Orchids.*

Brassia verrucosa 'Lucerne' AM/AOS—86 pts   **Stunning but long spikes**

ANYONE FOR ORCHIDS?

Window Box Greenhouse

An easy and inexpensive way to get started learning greenhouse techniques is to buy a window box greenhouse. These boxes come in a variety of standard sizes and are screwed to the window trim on the outside of the window.

The size can be the exact size of the window or bigger, if you don't mind putting up extra framing around your window and applying the window box to the framing. Make sure to caulk all around the frame of the window and the window box.

Window greenhouses come with a slanting roof that can be opened for ventilation and a screen to keep insects out of the house. Also included are plastic coated wire racks. It is a good idea to order an extra rack. It should be used on the floor of the greenhouse to give the plants some ventilation and to keep them from standing in water.

The supporting brackets for the racks have to be screwed into predrilled holes in the box. Where they go depends on the height of your plants and how much space you want between the shelves. You can order extra brackets and install them so that later you can move the racks without having to unscrew and move the old brackets. Make sure to install the racks so that the bent edge keeps the plants from falling off the shelf.

Instructions that come with the boxes state that the original house windows can be left in place. It is quite easy to remove them, and it gives you better access and a closer intimacy with your plants. It also prevents "cook outs" or "freeze outs" if the inside window is inadvertently closed.

The bottom of these boxes is generally made of some sort of paneling or fiberboard. Cover the panel with a sheet of fiberglass insulation, then a piece of bubble pack insulation. Next install the plastic tray that comes with the box. Use masking tape to install a thermostatically controlled heating cable to the tray. These cables are usually set to 75° and only are needed during the cold winter months. Next pour in a good supply of perlite or gravel, moisten it well and put in the extra rack upside down. This will allow about an inch of air space over the gravel and will keep the plants on the bottom shelf from standing in water.

One excellent accessory is a small low volume hi-fi fan. (Stores like Radio Shack stock them.) The gently moving air is of great benefit to the plants and helps distribute the humidity. Another accessory good for both plants and grower is a small cold water vaporizer. Run at least a few times during the cold weather when house humidity is very low.

Depending upon the exposure of the window shading of some sort will be necessary from March till October. Rolls of thin green plastic can be purchased. Cut them to fit the glass panels, moisten, and apply to the wet glass with a squeegee. Another method is to paint the glass with a very dilute solution of inexpensive latex paint (10 parts of water to one part paint). This mixture, though slightly less attractive, reflects the heat, as well as providing shading, and may be necessary in a south facing window.

You can also install a bamboo slat curtain or use plastic net shading. Of course, it is possible to remove all the plants, summer them outdoors and avoid the shading problem entirely.

In any case, once a year the plants should be removed for greenhouse cleaning. A solution of Phrysan (1 T. to one gallon of water) is used to wash off the inside of the glass. This removes algae and fungus of all kinds. The perlite should be removed and replaced. If the perlite is allowed to dry, it may be sucked up by a vacuum cleaner.

In the fall, in cold climates, the window box should be insulated by wrapping the entire box in bubble pack plastic and taped in place. Bubble pack is used to pack fragile objects for shipping and makes an excellent insulation. It comes in 24″ and 36″ widths. Contrary to your expectations it looks quite attractive from the inside, something like bottle glass windows.

During the dark winter months, it is very pleasant to light the window box either with a short fluorescent tube or a Plant Lite spot or two.

Because of the excellent light and cool winter temperatures almost any orchid will thrive in this environment. Try the easy list first and then progress to the moderate and difficult ones.

Light Growing

Growing orchids under lights is a fast growing and fun way of getting started with orchids. Supplementary natural window light with fluorescent tubes or "Grow-lite" spots is the most satisfactory because the combination of daylight and artificial

Orchids growing under lights

lights will make plants grow, flourish and bloom. If available window's area is limited then a light set-up is great.

How Does Light Make Plants Grow?

Without getting too technical here are a few basic facts and vocabulary used in light growing:

Phyto-illumination is the technical word for gardening by means of light. **Photosynthesis** is the growth process basic to plants. Carbon dioxide in the air combines with water and min-

Rows one and three are phalaenopsis grown under lights. Rows two and four are siblings grown in a greenhouse. The light grown plants are much better.

erals in the soil to form carbohydrates. This happens because of the action of light on chlorophyll, a substance found in all green plants.

Phytochrome is a chemical pigment found in plants. Discovered only three or four years ago, this pigment when acted upon by light, triggers growth changes from seed to fruit throughout the life of the plant. Red light energy activates this pigment, encouraging fast plant growth. It is a good idea to include special tubes like Grow-Lux or Vita-Lite which provide this type of light.

Photoperiod, light and dark, periods and their relative lengths have an effect on plant maturity. Actually, recent investigations have proven that it is not the length of day which affects growth, but the duration of the dark period which follows. Although many plants can grow under continuous light, nearly all plants prefer a dark period each day for normal growth. All plants need some darkness, periodically, to grow well or to trigger flowering. The ideal photoperiods of plants vary, some preferring long days and short nights, others the reverse, and some equal day/night periods.

ANYONE FOR ORCHIDS?

Light is measured in wave lengths. White or natural light is composed of and may be broken down into red, orange, yellow, green, blue, violet and ultraviolet. A good balanced lamp radiates all these wave lengths in the same proportion as outdoor sunlight.

The red energy triggers growth, maturity and flowering. However, too much red causes plants to become tall and "leggy." Blue light alone causes short stocky growth with fewer blossoms or no flowering at all. A proper balance of red and blue energy as well as the proper natural proportion of the other colors tend to produce normal healthy plants.

Although the green foliage of plants reflects much of the yellow and green light that falls on them, the benefits of "trace" light elements cannot be minimized and are very important to the total light required for good growth.

The closer your fluorescent tubes come to providing this full, broad spectrum of light the better. The problem of shock caused by moving plants from artifical sunlight to outdoors and back can be eliminated by using broad spectrum light.

Based on the wattage consumption (the electrical power you pay for) fluorescent lamps are about three times more efficient than incandescent bulbs in converting electrical energy into visible light energy.

To determine how much light a plant will require, one should consider where and how it grows best in natural environment.

High intensity light would be provided by a four lamp 40 watt fluorescent fixture located 12-18″ above the plants. This would light a plant area of 2′ × 5′.

Medium intensity light would be provided in the system above with lamps 16-30″ above the plants, or with a two lamp 40 watt fixture located 3-12″ above the plants. This would effectively light an area of 1¼′ × 5′.

Floral Cart

A floral cart can provide a small easily managed environment for orchids. These come knocked down but are easily assembled, giving a growing area of three shelves and each are 1½′ × 4′.

Floral carts come with an aluminum frame, three plastic trays, three sets of lights and 4″ heavy duty casters, so that it can be easily moved. A timer is needed to turn the lights on and off.

The trays are equipped with a drainage hole and plug, so that a flooded tray can be easily drained. These trays should be filled with white marble chips to best reflect the light and to provide a humid environment. Small pebbles are also practical. Fill the trays about 1½″ deep with the gravel.

The light fixtures hold four 48″ fluorescent tubes and four incandescent bulbs. This amount of illumination throws off a good deal of heat so it will be necessary to provide some small fans or blowers to help dissipate the heat and to help evaporate water surrounding the pebbles, thereby providing moisture and humidity.

Set your timer to 16 hours of daylight. This can be changed if you wish to fuss with providing seasons of the year.

To accomplish the change of season effect on your light grown plants, you can set up the following schedule:

16 hours of lighting, March through August.
15 hours of lighting, January, February, September and October.
14 hours of lighting, November and December.

Phalaenopsis lueddemanniana **Great under lights**   Photo by C. E. Poulsen

Even this small change in day-length will trigger bloom in photosensitive plants.

The easiest and most pleasing plants to grow in this kind of set-up are Paphopedilums. Since their growth habit is horizontal they benefit from the direct light from above. Vertically growing plants like Cattleyas do poorly because only the tips of the leaves are receiving sufficient illumination.

Phalaenopsis (also horizontal growth habit) do well but, of course, the long spikes of modern hybrids get tangled in the lights and are not too satisfactory. If you can content yourself with the charm of the small blooming species, you will be rewarded by an almost constant display of bloom.

Miniatures are a delight under lights and especially attractive because they are so accessible and visible on the cart and not lost in a "forest" of other plants in the greenhouse.

Basement Light Set Ups

If you have a basement available, it can be turned into a large growing area. A great deal of planning is required to make a really practical set up in a basement.

Here are a few pointers to help you get started.

Benching like that in a greenhouse is probably more practical than your old ping-pong table covered with perlite trays.

A floor drain is a necessity. You have no idea how much water pours through several hundred plants.

In a really big set-up, the ballasts (starters) from fluorescent tubes will generate so much heat that the area will be much too hot. Ballasts can be wired to long wires and be kept away from the growing area. Even so, it will probably be necessary to ventilate some of the heat through a basement window.

In any light set-up, sufficient humidity is a real problem especially if ventilation is going on. A really good cold water humidifier is a necessity. Plenty of moving air is a problem in a closed area like a basement and remember that too much blowing can dehydrate.

Plan for some lights to be set up vertically and you can illuminate the sides of tall growing plants like Cattleyas.

Paint your walls white for maximum reflection.

Build a good repotting area and make sure to include a sink and hose connection.

Stay away from your laundry area and your workshop. It won't hurt the plants but it will bother people who use them.

Caring For Your Light Grown Orchids

The same basic principles apply to light grown plants as to greenhouse with a few exceptions. Humidity is something of a problem. Misting often will help some, but make sure that the gravel in the trays is always wet.

Fertilizing programs should be slightly different. Since the plants are living in a constant environment, they need a very dilute feeding at every watering of approximately one part in 10,000 (100 ppm) of a balanced inorganic fertilizer, like Peters 18-18-18. An occasional switch to fish emulsion is beneficial.

As to pest control, Orthene is a good biodegradable low toxicity broad spectrum systemic. It is ideal for use in the house. A monthly application should take care of most insect

Phalaenopsis equestris 'Mary Noble' CCM/AOS—86 pts

Exhibited by Jack W. McQuerry

Loads of small flowers on small plant—easy grower

Paph sukhakulii 'Jeannette' HCC/AOS—76 pts
Exhibited by Stan & Jeanette Brachrar
Great under lights

problems. If plants are summered out of doors, dip them in a solution of Malathion before bringing them back in the house.

Fungus is sometimes a problem indoors, as is algae on pebbles. A dilute solution of Physan 20 (1 T. to one gallon of water) will solve these problems.

Red spider mites are the worst threat to indoor gardening. They thrive in dry air. Spray regularly with the miticide, Kelthane. Only a miticide will kill them. Keep the growing area moist and mist the plants often.

Laelia pumila 'Steven Bloch' CCM/AOS—83 pts
Exhibited by Robert K. Wolf
Compact plant

The following list of plants will give you an idea of the wide range of plants that will thrive in a floral cart or basement set-up:

Aerangis species	moderate
Angraecum eichlerianum	moderate
Angraecum philippinense	difficult
Ascondenda hybrids	easy
Ascocentrum miniatum	easy
Ascocentrum pumila	moderate
Aspasia epidendroides	easy
Aspasia lunata	easy
Broughtonia sanguinea	easy
Catasetums	moderate
Cattleya hybrids	moderate
Cattleya luteola	moderate
Cattleya forbesii	easy
Cirrhopetalums	easy
Cynoches chlorochilon	moderate
Cynoches loddigesii	moderate
Dendrobium antennatum	moderate

31

ANYONE FOR ORCHIDS?

Dendrobium jenkensii	difficult
Dendrobium leonis	difficult
Dendrobium linguiforme	easy
Dendrobium mannii	moderate
Dendrobium phalaenopsis	easy
Dendrobium rigidum	moderate
Doritaenopsis	easy
Epidendrum cochleatum	easy
Epidendrum mariae	moderate
Eria fragans	easy
Gastrochilus calceolare	moderate
Gastrochilus dasypogon	moderate
Gomesa recurva	moderate
Haraella ordorata	difficult
Laelia pumila	difficult
Laelia (rupiculous species)	moderate
Leptotes bicolor	easy
Leptotes unicolor	easy
Neofinetia falcata	easy
Oncidium (equitant species and hybrids)	easy
Oncidium Kalihi	difficult
Oncidium longipes	difficult
Oncidium ornithorhyncum	moderate
Ornithocephalus species	easy
Paphiopedilum species and hybrids	easy, moderate and difficult
Phalaenopsis hybrids	easy
Phalaenopsis cornu-cervi	easy
Phalaenopsis equestris	easy
Phalaenopsis hieroglyphica	easy
Phalaenopsis lueddemanniana	easy
Phalaenopsis mannii	easy
Phalaenopsis schilleriana	easy
Phalaenopsis violacea	moderate
Phragmipedium caudatum	moderate
Phragmipedium schlimii	difficult
Polyrrhizia funalis	difficult
Rodriguezia species	moderate
Saccolabium species	moderate
Sarcochilus species	moderate

Trichopilia species	moderate
Vascostylis	moderate
Zygopetalum crinitum	easy

Each name on this list is followed by an evaluation of the ease with which these plants will grow under lights. Beginners should start with the easy plants and add the moderate and difficult types as their growing skills expand.

Photo by Charles Marden Fitch

Zygopetalum crinitum
Marvelous fragrance

33

C. Breckinridge Snow 'Susan
Lynn Rose' AM/AOS—81 pts

Miltonia Hoggar X Anjou

Notylia mirabilis

II
Getting Started

Join your local orchid society. You can find out when and where they meet from the American Orchid Society, Inc., Botanical Museum of Harvard University, Cambridge, Mass. 02138. While you're at it, join the American Orchid Society; you will receive a subscription of the AOS Bulletin. If requested, they will send you a list of their other publications and many excellent books on the subject of Orchids.

Most local societies have a monthly meeting. Often the meeting includes the club business, a lecture or slide program and refreshments. During the refreshments, you get a chance to chit chat with the members. Many clubs have a sales table. Members bring in divisions of plants for sale. You may be able to pick up an extra nice plant.

The best part of the meeting may well be the Show Table. Members bring in their blooming plants for display and judging. The Show Table is grouped into divisions according to the size of the greenhouse. That way, growers with small houses do not have to compete with big growers or commercial growers. Usually there is a class for window sill growers and light growers. Often the plants are judged, a discussion follows, perhaps telling how the plant was grown or something of its parents. You get a chance to see plants you've read about in catalogues, articles and advertisements.

The society may also sponsor a display in a local flower show or even in a mall or bank. This activity is loads of fun and work, but it's a grand way to get to know the other members.

Hopefully, the society will feature workshops and visits or tours of each other's greenhouses. They well may own a library and lend books to members.

After you have joined your local society, ask to visit some members' greenhouses. Every greenhouse is different but there is something useful to learn everywhere. When you get there, try not to look only at the plants. Look at the benches, the heating, humidifier, shading, watering, hoses, etc. See how plants are arranged. Not everything you see will apply to your own conditions but keep an open mind. Make notes or sketches and ask questions.

Your First Plants

Where do you get your first plants? Perhaps a friend has given you a plant. Maybe you have seen them in a local nursery. However you get them, you need to know their names and their needs. Never buy an unnamed plant unless it is a species and you think you can figure out at least what genera it is. Then, if you can bloom it and refer to botanical descriptions or an expert to find its full name. Unnamed hybrids are virtually valueless. Unnamed plants cannot be shown. Half the fun of growing orchids is learning about their origins and geneology.

Most orchids can be grouped for growing purposes into three temperature categories.

Warm Orchids such as Phalaenopsis. Orchids from low lying, hot tropical climates, fall into this category. They like day temperatures of 75° and above and night temperatures of 65°-75°.

Intermediate Orchids such as Cattleyas. These flourish in moderate elevations with day temperatures of 70° and night temperatures of 55°-65°.

Cool Orchids like Odontoglossums come from high mountain areas usually bathed in misty clouds. They require day temperatures of 60°-70° and night temperatures of 45°-50°.

Keep in mind your conditions when buying your first plants. Until you have really accumulated lots of experience in growing orchids, you should not try plants whose needs you can't meet.

Many modern hybrids are so complex that these plants are less fussy about temperatures. Modern hybridizers have "warmed up" the cool growing Odonts and Miltonias by breeding them with species from warmer areas. Miniature Cymbidiums for instance are intermediate through Standard (big) Cymbidiums are cool.

If you have joined your local Orchid Society, you will have immediate access to good plants. Most growers have divisions to give or sell. It's not a bad idea to learn to grow on less valuable plants. Don't invest in an awarded plant until you know you can handle it. However, do try to buy a plant in good growing condition. Seedlings and back bulbs are not for you.

Try to buy a Paph with several growths. Buy front divisions of Cattleyas. Look for plants starting into new growth. Make sure that they are well or newly potted and ready to go.

Cattleya bowringiana Exhibited by Rodney Wilcox Jones **An easy grower—even on a window sill**

ANYONE FOR ORCHIDS?

Some of the members of your local society will be commercial growers. Make an appointment, be ready to listen and learn, and ask for their recommendations. Most orchidists will not sell you tricky or rare plants.

Of course, you have joined the American Orchid Society and are getting the AOS Bulletin. Most people keep these bulletins for years, often having them bound. Articles, that are over your head now, may be just the ticket a few months from now. The back of the bulletin is packed with ads for supplies and plants. What should you do? First of all, send off for a lot of catalogues. Most catalogues have marvelous pictures and descriptions, even tips on growing. For instance, Jones and Scully in Miami, Florida, lists plants for growing under lights, miniatures, fragrant orchids, cool growers, etc. These lists are really helpful. Often you will find "combination offerings" at reduced prices. These are a good deal for a beginner. Perhaps you can buy three Cattleyas, one white, one yellow, one lavender. Often you will find special offerings of a "Plant-a-Month." Actually, this may work out quite well because you will receive plants ready to bloom at all seasons.

Until you are confident about handling mature plants, hold off on seedlings. Small ones may be years from blooming. But every collector eventually turns to buying young plants. It's a great thrill to see the first bloom.

Don't load up only one genus. Try Cattleyas, Laelias, Epidendrums, Oncidiums and Miniature Cymbidiums if you have an intermediate house. See how you do with them. In the first place, sticking to just Cattleyas or just Cymbidiums makes for a dull collection and a look of sameness. A varied collection will astonish your friends. Most people don't realize how different orchid blooms can be.

If you live near an advertiser in the AOS Bulletin, by all means, go to see him. You will be offered good plants at fair prices and you will learn a lot by seeing his set-up and by listening to what he has to say. There is a lot to be said for buying something and seeing what you're getting.

Most orchid societies hold auctions for fund raising. It gives members a chance to buy a division of a plant they have seen and admired on the show table.

If you are lucky, the society has printed and distributed a list. This gives you a chance to do some research. You can check off those plants you know about. Everyone gets "auction fever" and, all warnings to the contrary, plunge right in over their heads, from time to time. But, do try to restrain yourself. Don't be the first to bid; wait a bit. Know exactly how much that plant costs in a catalogue. Beginners always go for things in bloom. Often the flowers are almost over and you've paid extra for something you don't get. Get to the auction early enough to look at the plants. A plant that looks great way up there in the front of the auditorium may not look so good when you get it home. Try to sit near someone you know and pick his brain if you are in doubt. If the plant is big, perhaps you can share it between two or three of you.

However you get your plants, through friends, commercial growers, ads, catalogues, or auctions, try to buy plants that give you flowers at all seasons of the year.

Some Cattleyas bloom more than once a year. Some bloom in season. Most Phalanopsis bloom in the spring. Cymbidiums start in the fall and go on through spring. Catalogues tell you whether a Cymbidium is early (fall), middle (winter) or late (spring). Find out about the expected bloom period of plants trying not to buy three or four purple Cattleyas all blooming in the fall.

One word of advice on the subject of plant size. Everyone loves big splashy plants. Nothing is more glamorous than a huge Cattleya or Cymbidium. There is something to be said for an enormous specimen plant. But a small greenhouse is quickly filled with big plants. Why not grow a specimen miniature instead. Three Ascodenda hybrids can be grown in the space required for one Vanda and the Ascodendas will bloom several times a year. Sure, *Angraecum sesquipedal* is a fabulous greenish Christmas star but *Angraecum philippinense* has a big flower on a small plant and loads of charm. Miltonias are an ideal example of the art of the hybridizer. Miltonias have a small attractive vegetative habit with wonderfully showy bright flowers.

Ascocentrum miniatum CBM/AOS—82 points **Never gets too big to manage**
 Alberts and Merkel
Angraecum philippinense 'Dorothy Wolf'—81 pts Exhibited by Robert K. Wolf
 A superb miniature for collectors

In a small greenhouse, every inch of space counts. You don't have room for big rangy plants with little tiny flowers. The ideal collection should have wide variety of flower shapes, sizes and colors.

Renanopsis Lena Ronold 'Madge Fordyce' CCM/AOS
Owner: Nico Lek de Tachinville
A fabulous plant but hardly suitable for the hobby grower in a small greenhouse

41

Photo by John C. Krau

Ascocentrum ampullaceum 'Bill Teel' AM/AOS—81 pts Exhibited by Bill Teel
Bright flowers on a smallish plant

The following list of plants are among the easiest orchids to grow. They are not fool-proof but almost everyone has learned on these:

Angraecum veitchii
Ansellia africana
Ascodenda hybrids
Brassavola nodosa
Brassia verrucosa
Cattleya bowringiana
Cattleya intermedia
Cattleya skinneri
Cattleya hybrids
Cymbidium Flirtation (miniature
Cymbidium Showgirl

Paphiopedilum Snowram 'Georgia' HCC/AOS
Penn Valley Orchids

Dendrobium kingianum
Dendrobium nobile
Dendrobium phalaenopsis hybrids
Doritaenopsis hybrids
Epidendrum alatum
Epidendrum cochleatum
Epidendrum fragrans
Epiphronitis veitchii
Eria fragrans
Laelia anceps
Maxillaria tenuifolia
Neofinetia falcata
Oncidium flexuosum
Oncidium sphacelatum
Oncidium varicosum
Ornithocephalus biconis

Paphiopedilum Maudiae
Paphiopedilum sukhakulii
Paphiopedilum venustum
Paphiopedilum St. Albans
Paphiopedilum insigne
Phalaenopsis cornu-cervi
Phalaenopsis equestris
Phalaenopsis hieroglyphica
Phalaenopsis lueddemanniana
Phalaenopsis mannii
Phalaenopsis hybrids
Rhynchostylis coelestis
Rhyncostylis retusa
Vanda cristata
Vanda hookerana
Zygopetalum species

Rhycostylis coelestes 'Hyacinth' AM/AOS
A handsome plant for high light

III
Greenhouse Building

Planning Greenhouses

Buying and building a greenhouse is an important and possibly expensive project. It is almost as important as buying a house or a car. Careful planning is a must. One of the first things to do is to visit as many greenhouses as possible.

Visit your friends and members of societies and really talk over their experiences. Make the rounds of your local garden centers to see if they have assembled models. Get the feel of the size, construction materials and foundations.

Greenhouse Note slatted benches, brick floor, glass to ground construction, open ventilation

Look up "Greenhouses" in the Yellow Pages. Often you can get a salesman to come over and advise you as to site, size and costs.

It is a good idea to send away for the literature available from various greenhouse manufacturers. They will send specifications on size, type, costs, heating and cooling requirements. Read and compare carefully. At the end of this chapter you will find a chart of the features of various commercially available greenhouse manufacturers and their names and addresses.

Site and Size

The size of course depends on the pocket book and the available space, but no one ever has enough space. Many models can be added to later on, which is a decided advantage.

The site depends so much on your property and the way your house is situated. Make sure that your greenhouse has good light all year round. You must have at least 3–4 hours of unobstructed sun as a bare minimum. Plot the shadows of your house and the trees both summer and winter taking into account the low angle of the sun in winter. Be wary of a lean-to facing west that will get overheated in summer.

Potting Shed or Work Room

Again, no one ever has enough space for repotting and storage of all the paraphernalia, associated with greenhouses. The inclusion of a work room and potting area is an often neglected feature. It is certainly worth the effort. One of the easiest solutions is to install a kitchen unit complete with cabinets and sink. A deep laundry tub is extremely useful. Greenhouse work is messy and few housewives are willing to use their kitchens for this purpose.

Building Codes and Permits

Check with your local government to see what restrictions and permits there may be in your locality. Make sure that you comply to the laws and all work is inspected. It is also a good idea to find out in advance about hook-up charges and monthly costs from your local utilities office.

Greenhouse and work area
Note fiberglass roof, gravel floor, garbage cans for potting
mix

Foundations

The question of foundations is more important than it may
seem evident at first. Many pre-fabricated greenhouses advertise
that no foundations are needed. All greenhouses must be se-
curely anchored to the ground and they must be level. A good
foundation will also prevent rotting of the greenhouse. In areas
of high wind or freezing in winter, a substantial foundation is
necessary. This would include a poured concrete or cement
block construction. Perhaps if the greenhouse is to be placed on
an existing concrete patio, it may be bolted down. The advice
of your local building department or a good contractor will save
headaches.

47

ANYONE FOR ORCHIDS?

Electrical and Water Hookup

Do not forget the all important electrical hookup, hot and cold water and heating arrangements. Often times these lines can be run from the house. Check with your plumber to see if your house heating capacity can be extended to the greenhouse. Unless you want to "get away from it all" a telephone extension is a nicety. Do run your electrical wire through conduit and use capped plugs and a covered light fixture. Regular wiring will not do in a greenhouse because of the danger of short circuits and fire. Make sure that you have enough electrical outlets. Extension cords are a "no-no" in a greenhouse. You will need outlets for humidistats, humidifier, exhaust louver motor and exhaust fan or turbulator as well as any extra small fans you may wish to add. The heater will be wired into the circuit directly but it is nice to have some flexibility. A licensed electrician can help you plan for all the outlets and connections you need.

Gas Heater with controls

Controls on a "back porch greenhouse"
Note: wire screen shelves, florescent fixtures, hose extender

49

Heating

Weather conditions vary so widely that you will need to consult an expert. You must figure degree days and size of greenhouse. You must also take into consideration your site, wind exposure and so on, in order to figure how many B.T.U. you need.

Probably the best type of heat for a greenhouse is hot water fin-tubing running around the perimeter of the greenhouse. This can be provided by your house heater if its capacity is great enough. There are gas fired hot water heaters and, of course, electric. The least desirable for orchids is a forced air system. However you heat your greenhouse, you should have a back-up system for emergency power failures. See section under Alarms.

Greenhouse Types

Greenhouses come in many different shapes and constructions. There are so many choices available that choosing may be difficult.

Greenhouses may be free-standing or attached to the house. An attached greenhouse offers the advantage of accessibility. It may also become an important architectural addition. It will also save some heat because of its being exposed on only three sides. It may be even span or lean to.

Greenhouses are either *built up* or *glass to ground*. Built up greenhouses have a solid wall to bench height. Glass to ground has sides down to the ground. There is a heat saving in the built up models but the areas under the benches are unusable, unless lighted by fluorescent tubes.

Other shapes are curved eave, straight sides, A-frame, geodesic dome, sphere, octagon, and Quonset hut styles.

Coverings

The coverings run the gamut from the classical glass to polyethylene, vinyl plastic and fiberglass.

Glass, of course, lets in all light, is expensive, more difficult to install and is a good conductor of heat and cold.

The polyethylene and vinyl plastics are inexpensive but not very durable, and have to be replaced as they weather. Some plastics have been processed with chemical additives that resist damage by ultraviolet light but are more expensive.

Fiberglass has the advantage of non-breakability, ease of construction and low heat conductance. It eventually does weather and must be replaced about every ten years. One good point is that fiberglass has the excellent property of light diffusion so that plants are bathed in light from all directions.

Cooling Systems

Virtually all greenhouses need some sort of cooling during the summer months and even on hot bright days in winter. In cool summer areas, ventilation with hand operated venting may suffice.

Basically, the principles of cooling are simple though methods vary. First, heat buildup can be lessened by shading. Second, you can cool the air by opening vents and letting hot air escape or by bringing in cooler outside air by the use of an exhaust fan. Third, you can cool by drawing air through an evaporative cooler. Climate, construction and location of your greenhouse dictates which type of cooling is for you.

Window box greenhouses present one of the most difficult challenges to cooling. Because the area is so small, the heat can build up in a matter of minutes. An exhaust fan with a thermostat can be set up to bring in cooler air from the house. If the house is air conditioned, so much the better.

The fan can be a squirrel cage blower rated at about 50 cfm (cubic feet per minute) or a kitchen or bathroom exhaust fan. The following diagram shows how to wire the fan and thermostat:

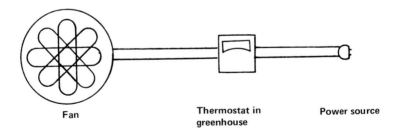

Fan   Thermostat in   Power source
             greenhouse

Figure 1

Another way to keep a window box cool is to install a roller blind with a shade cloth on the outside of the window. This is quite effective and works even in the event of a power failure.

You can make this awning yourself from a window shade roller and commercial shade cloth. Greenhouse supply companies can provide this shading cloth in various degrees of shading—60%, 70% and 80%. If you have difficulty obtaining shade cloth, heavy cheese cloth or white netting will do.

White cloth has the advantage of reflecting heat.

Mount the roller on the house above the window box. Put hooks at the bottom of the greenhouse to anchor the shade. This apparatus will work better if a dead air space of 2 or 3″ is maintained between the house and the shade.

Many window greenhouses come equipped with a hinged top. You can easily install a thermal piston to open and close this top, thereby letting out the air (not practical to use with an awning). A thermal piston is filled with a material that expands when the temperature goes up. The piston is attached to a lever which pushes the window open. When the temperature falls, the material on the piston contracts, thereby lowering the window vent. This piston can be adjusted to various temperatures from 60°F (15C) and 100°F (38C). It is probably a good idea to set a small window box at 70° so that the fast heat buildup does not overtake the unit.

If you don't mind looking out at a really green world, you can apply green polyethylene sheeting directly to the outside wet glass. Press down with a squeegee. This sheeting will not stick on the aluminum frame so you must cut out each section to fit the panes. This material provides approximately 65% shading.

There is a relatively new product out that can be used in much the same way except that it is applied on the inside. This is the new solar-reflecting plastic being used in store windows. It reflects up to 80% of the infra-red heat waves and is usually made of polyester film that has been treated with vaporized aluminum. It does tend to crack with age.

Lean-to greenhouses should probably be equipped with an exhaust fan. This fan should be mounted on one side of the house near the roof. Near the floor on the opposite side install a louvered intake. This arrangement will help bring in cooler air at near ground level and push out the hot air near the roof. Thermostatic control of this system works the same as for Figure 1. Make sure that you procure a greenhouse thermostat because it will be made of corrosion resistant material to withstand the humidity in a greenhouse.

The intake louver can be purchased with a motor attached and then should be wired to the thermostat along with the fan so that they operate together. Make sure your exhaust fan is of sufficient capacity to cool your size greenhouse. The following table will help:

TABLE 1

Size of fan	Cfm rating	Size of house
7"	135	6 × 8
10"	520	8 × 10
12"	650	8 × 12
18"	1,625	8 × 16

In very hot weather or an exposed site, this fan may operate continuously all day. If you have a screen in the door, leave it open and disconnect the intake louver motor. This saves some energy and prolongs the motor life. Of course, in spring, winter and fall, it must be reinstalled.

Along with the air cooling, it will be necessary to use some sort of shading on the outside to prevent direct rays from burning the plants. Rollup shades of bamboo, redwood slats, aluminum blinds or saran cloth are available. They can be raised or lowered by hand or automatically with an electric motor and photoelectric cell. In exposed areas and particularly with orchid plants, it will probably be necessary to leave the shading on all summer from March–October.

Of course, many people use the other types of shading mentioned in regard to window greenhouses. White wash is quite inexpensive and though messy to apply, does eventually weather away especially in frost areas and particularly after a snowfall.

An easy substitute for the commercially available white wash is a solution made with 10 parts of water to 1 part of cheap latex house paint. It does not weather away as well as white wash. Do not use on plexiglass.

Don't forget that, in a lean-to, it is often possible to open the door to the house and benefit from the larger air volume or any existing air conditioning.

ANYONE FOR ORCHIDS?

Of course, air conditioning can be installed in the greenhouse by using a wet pad evaporative cooler. This apparatus is applicable to both lean-to and free standing models.

The evaporative cooler consists of a metal water reservoir outside the greenhouse on the ground. It contains an electrical motor, a circulatory pump, a suction blower and the wet pads of aspen fiber. The blower draws the warm air in through the fiber pads. As the water evaporates, it cools the air which is then blown back into the house. At the same time, the exhaust fan is blowing hot air out at the ridge. Both of these pieces of equipment are wired to the same thermostat and work together. In hot dry climates, this works quite well and actually lowers the heat 20–30°. However, in humid climates, the efficiency is greatly diminished and is probably not worthwhile.

Very much on the same order but particularly for free standing models is a wet pad installed in the side or end of the house wall. Of course, it must be taken down during the heating season in colder climates. The aspen pad becomes the wall of the house and is kept wet by a perforated drip pipe running along the top of the pad. There is a gutter at the bottom so that the water is returned to the reservoir and a pump which keeps circulating the water. Again, there is the exhaust fan to pull air through the moist pad and to push the hot air out. You must not leave any vents or doors open because all the air should be drawn through the pads. You need 1 sq. ft. of pad for every 150 cfm of fan velocity. For example, a 10 X 20 house needs an 18″ fan so 1650 cfm divided by 150 = 10.8 sq. ft. of pad.

Refer to Table 1 to figure the pad size required for your greenhouse.

In areas where evaporation coolers are not efficient a Fan Jet cooler can be installed in large free standing greenhouses. This equipment is adequate for houses up to 100′ in length. It consists of a motorized shutter hot air exhaust fan and a long perforated plastic tube running the length of the house near the roof. This unit is, of course, triggered by a thermostat which opens the shutter, and the exhaust fan pulls this cool outside air into the Fan Jet tube. The air escapes through the holes in the tube dropping down all through the greenhouse and then is pulled out by the exhaust. The distribution of air is particularly good for orchids.

Since orchids benefit so much from moist moving air, a humidifier with a fan is an ideal item for a small house.

Misting the house with an attachment on the hose is an excellent method for cooling but requires the grower to be home. Turbulators are also available to keep the air moving inside the greenhouse. They look like an old fashioned ceiling fan with bent blades. A spray mister head with a humidistat can be installed on the floor under the benches and when aided by a floor fan the results are excellent.

These humidifiers can be set up by your plumber by running a tap from the cold water line. A float valve inside keeps them filled and they are best installed into a humidistat.

Photo by Carl Webber

Humidifier and humidistat (note electrical conduit and extra fan)

Now that you have your greenhouse set up, heated and ventilated, and provisions made for potting, you need to give consideration to the floor.

If the greenhouse was placed on an already existing terrace, patio or concrete slab, make sure that provision is made for water run off. There is a lot in a greenhouse.

If, on the other hand, the foundation was poured in an excavated area, you now have a clay floor. This should be filled with at least 6-8″ of gravel. Too thin a depth will lead to a frozen floor. Some growers swear by large cut stones. Others use pea gravel or rolled river stones. All these stones help to impede the travel of snails. They are, of course, hard to keep clean and this is necessary. Raking helps so that small bits of debris settle down between the stones. Many growers dislike this mess, especially in lean-to greenhouses, where dirt can be tracked into the house. Other solutions are flagstones (very expensive and very slick) and bricks set on sand. Algae loves bricks and must be cleaned off, but brick floors do drain well. Concrete or tile floors are wonderfully easy to keep clean but must be engineered perfectly with excellent floor draining so that water does not form into puddles.

Next comes the benches. One has only to visit other greenhouses to be aware of the variety of solutions to this vexing problem. They must be at the right height and not too deep for you to reach to the back. They must be rot resistant (redwood or cedar) and never treated with wood preserver which is very toxic to plants. They must allow for the free passage of air and water. Solid plank benches are an abomination to orchids. They must have a lip or edge to prevent plants from tipping over and falling to the ground. And, they must be terribly strong to hold up all that weight.

Wire benches with wooden frames are expensive but easy to build. Wire can be used with galvanized pipes which are sunk in concrete footings.

One of the best benches I have ever seen incorporates plastic egg crate ceiling tiles. This is beautiful, light, clean and white and helps to diffuse and reflect light. It is very expensive.

If your greenhouse is glass to ground, you may wish to build low benches like a trundle bed to slip under the main benches. Do not put plants on the floor. Slugs and bush snails get in, and there is no air circulation under them.

If you have a builtup greenhouse, you may wish to have fluorescent light fixtures installed over the low benches. Make sure they are shielded from the cascades of water which pour on them from above. Use clear fiberglass.

Step benches are available and not too hard to build. However, they can only be used against a flat wall. Curving greenhouses cannot accommodate step benches. The narrow glass shelving available with many greenhouses for installation near the top of the wall is not too good a place to put orchids. Wire

Stepped staging permits easier access to the plants and
better light and air

can be substituted for the glass.

Your plumber has hopefully installed hot and cold water. You
will need an excellent quality hose because you will use it so
often. You must compromise between weight and strength. Do
not buy a small capacity hose that will make your watering
chores too long. If your greenhouse is small, cut the hose to fit
the space. Nothing is more annoying than dragging around coils
of excess hose.

You will also need at least one water wand. This is an aluminum hose extender with a bend in the end. Pick one that will
reach to the back of the benches and to the pots overhead. They
come in several lengths.

Buy yourself a good quality water breaker, but be resigned to
the fact that salt water builds up in them and they must be replaced. A brass mister (fine or extra fine) is a real necessity.
Orchids have to be misted early in the morning. Both the mister
and the breaker screw right into the hose extender.

Now for fertilizing, you need something more than a watering can. You can buy a small inexpensive gadget called a Hozon. It works by syphoning up a solution of fertilizer and mixing it with the water running through the hose, thereby watering and fertilizing at the same time. It consists of a brass hose fitting that is inserted between the faucet and the hose. Attached to this fitting is a rubber hose and a springlike filter. This hose is placed in a bucket of fertilizer, dissolved in water. The proportions to use come with the gadget. It can be used with either inorganic fertilizers or with fish emulsion solutions.

Another, but very expensive gadget, is a Proportioner. This is a pump that is placed on the water line between the faucet and hose and it, too, draws up dissolved fertilizer. Its great advantage is that the pump keeps the solution evenly distributed even though your water pressure varies or the delivery hose is bent. This way, you are sure that every plant gets the same amount of fertilizer.

Alarm System

An indispensable addition to your greenhouse equipment is an alarm system.

Every alarm system has three elements: a sensing device, the alarm device and a power source.

The sensing device has to determine when the temperature has fallen too low. A home heating thermostat will do the trick. It must be the type that has electrical contacts that close when the low temperature is reached. Consult the Yellow Pages under Heating and Air Conditioning, Furnace Supplies and Thermostats.

The alarm device can be a bell, buzzer, lights or door chime. It must be capable of operating on a six volt battery.

The power source is a six volt battery. Also used is an ordinary toggle system.

Figure 2 shows the diagram for wiring up this system.

It is very helpful to know if the electricity supplied by the public utility has failed, since this has the effect of turning off most alarms, heating and cooling devices. The circuit shown in Figure 3 provides such a 'fail safe' alarm. When the elecelectricity fails, the relay circuit falls into its "normally" closed position. This connects the six volt battery to the bell or other alarm device. Being awakened by such an alarm at 2 a.m. on a

Thermostat   **Bell**   **Switch**   **Battery**

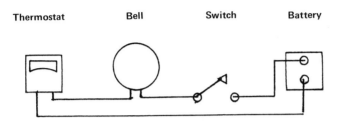

freezing winter night is one of the orchid growers more exciting experiences.

There are several methods of alternative heating. You can keep on hand a "salamander" fired by kerosene, or a portable propane heater. If your greenhouse is free standing you can light a charcoal fire in your outdoor grill or even build a charcoal fire in large clay pots. The charcoal fumes are poisonous so you can not stay in the greenhouse while they are being used. If all else fails you can lug all your plants into the house and build a fire in your fireplace.

Flooding the floor with hot water (if you have it) will keep the temperature up while you fix the heater or if the power failure is not too prolonged.

In the summer if your power fails and the temperature goes up over 100°, open all vents by hand, prop open the door, and mist the plants every half hour until the emergency is over or the temperature outside drops. At least as many plants are killed by "cookouts" as by "freeze outs."

You can also include an intrusion device that breaks the circuits when the door is opened. This is mounted on the door and frame.

Only the thermostat needs to be in the greenhouse. The rest can be in any convenient place in your home.

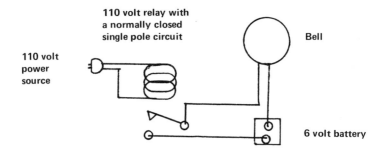

110 volt relay with
a normally closed
single pole circuit

Bell

110 volt
power
source

6 volt battery

Laelia anceps

List of Greenhouse Fabricators

B. C. Greenhouse Builders Ltd., 7425 Hedley Av., Burnaby, BC, Canada V5E 2R1. Traditional-style aluminum structures. Includes two roof vents. Four styles available, two lean-to models. $445–$980.

Botanical Environments, 1044 Pioneer Way, Suite C, El Cajon, CA 92020. Lightweight (33 pounds), low cost ($69.95) Gro-Dome. Dome is 7' high, approximately 11' in diameter.

W. Atlee Burpee Co., Warminster, PA 18974. English Greenhouse, offered by the famous seed company. Traditional style, has gutters and condensation channels. Four models, two lean-to styles. $585–$785.

Casaplanta, 16129 Runnymede St., Van Nuys, CA 91406. Plastic tube frame, curved-eave style. Includes four redwood shelves. Small (7' high, 4' wide, 3' deep) and ligthweight. $89.95.

Environmental Dynamics, Box 996, Sunnymead, CA 92388. Five models, traditional or curved-eave styles, redwood or steel frames, Hydroponic kits and double-walled insulation available. $89.95–$744.50.

Everlite, R. T. Nolan, Box 432, Des Plaines, IL 60018. Aluminum struc-curved-eave style. Eight models and all sizes. $350–$4,000.

Four Seasons Greenhouse Co., 17 Ave. of Americas, New York, NY 10013. Aluminum frames. Traditional and curved eave styles. Double-walled insulation. Seventy styles and sizes. $449–$2,349.

Gothic Arch Greenhouses, Box 1564, Mobile, AL 36001. Curved-eave design. Four sizes available, hobby to commercial, $649.40–$2,760.20.

Hansen Weather Port, 313 N. Taylor, Gunnison, CO 81230. Quonset-hut style. Galvanized steel frame. Seven sizes. Exhaust fan included. $285–$665.

Janco Greenhouses, J. A. Nearing Co., 9390 Davis Av., Laurel, MD 20810. Straight or curved eaves, aluminum framing, built-up or glass-to-ground. Nine hobby models, many sizes, including commercial. $600–$4,000.

Lord and Burnham, Irvington, NY 10533. All sizes and shapes, hobby to commercial, built-up or glass-to-ground. Insured for one year against wind or hail damage. $585–$5,527.

McGregor Greenhouses, 1195 Thompson Av., Santa Cruz, CA 95063. Traditional-styled, redwood frame. Two models with add-on attachments. $159.95–$368.95.

National Greenhouse Company, Box 100, Pana, IL 62557. Features three models, variety of sizes. Dutch-design. Redwood and pipe bench supplied with the Eaglet or glass-to-ground models. $762–$3,395.

Edward Owen Engineering, Snow Shoe, PA 16874. Aluminum frames, traditional-styled. Safety glass panes butted together. Gutters and downspouts included. Four sizes. $795–$1,095.

Pacific Coast Greenhouse Manufacturing Co., 430 Hurlingame Av., Redwood City, CA 94063. Treated redwood structures, traditional styling. Comes in 3-foot add-on sections. Four models, 19 sizes. $356–$8,241.

ANYONE FOR ORCHIDS?

Plant Works, Tiffany Industries, Inc., 145 Weldon Parkway, Maryland Heights, MO 63043. Hydroponic greenhouses. Three styles. Quonset-hut, traditional and lean-to, add-on sections. Crystal Gardens model features geodesic-style panels. $690–$2,998.

Redi-Bilt Greenhouses, Ripa Industries, 112 N College Rd., Wilmington, NC 28401. Cedar trim comes in green, white, red or brown. Three models, traditional styles with built-up sides, and six sizes. $375–$1,495.

Peter Reimuller—The Greenhouseman, 980 17th Av., Santa Cruz, CA 95062. Three models, several sizes. Dutch-design, curved or straight-eave styling. Redwood or aluminum frames. $119.95–$679.95.

Santa Barbara Greenhouses, 390 Dawson Dr., Camarillo, CA 93010. Redwood frame, straight-eave style. Two styles, eight sizes. $168–$412.50.

Semispheres, Box 26273, Richmond, VA 23260. Geodesic domes. Salt-treated pine frames. Seven models. Ceiling fan included with some sizes. $139–$14,375.

Shelter Dynamics, Inc., Box 616, Round Rock, TX 78664. Features the Solarsphere. Clear or opaque panels available. Frame comes in brown, green or yellow-gold, 8½' high, 14' in diameter. $995.

Solar Technology Corp., 2160 Clay St., Denver, CO 80211. Features Solar Garden, sun-heated greenhouses, high south wall style or lean-to. Add-on sections available. $1,400–$3,440.

Sturdi-built Manufacturing Co., 11304 SW Boones Ferry Rd., Portland, OR 97219. Unusual and unique designs, A-frame, traditional and gazebo. Nine styles, many sizes. $485–$2,415.

Sun Greenhouses, Box 687, Chatham, NJ 07928. Traditional styling. Aluminum frames. Freestanding or lean-to models. Gutters included. Prices start at $379.

Sun/America Corp., Box 125, Houston, TX 77001. Aluminum frames, traditional styles. Shelving included. Seven models, one indoor-outdoor. $99.95–$279.95.

Sun-Glo Greenhouses, 3714 S Hudson, Seattle, WA 98118. Double-walled, curved-eave styles with tinted covering. Aluminum frame. Aluminum benches included. Two styles and standard sizes or custom-ordered sizes. $395–$2,250.

Texas Greenhouse Co., 2717 St. Louis Av., Ft. Worth, TX 76110. Redwood or aluminum frames. Double strength glass covering. Traditional, Dutch-design or curved-eave styling. Twelve models and many sizes. $580–$5,362.

Turner Greenhouses, Box 1260, Goldsboro, NC 27530. Steel framing. Dutch-design styles. Three models, or will make to specifications. Add-on sections available. $131–$1,591.

Vegetable Factory Greenhouses, 100 Court St., Copiague, NY 17726. Double-walled construction. Shatterproof covering. Dutch-design shapes. Two styles, four sizes. $499–$998.

Water Works Gardenhouses, Box 905, El Cerrito, CA 94350. Features Produce-R model, hydroponic greenhouses. Redwood frame. Four sizes. Greenhouse available alone. $600–$3,000.

I V
Supplies

Potting Mixes

It is a good idea to make up and keep on hand several kinds of orchid growing mixes. An easy beginners' mix (which I still use) is 2/3 fir bark, 1/3 tree fern and 1/3 perlite. It can be made using small and medium grade bark and tree fern. Use small for paphs and seedlings, medium for everything else. The following mixes listed in Table 2 are quite satisfactory. If some of the ingredients such as fritted potash are not available, they can be eliminated.

If you decide to make up your mixes, they should be stored in small plastic garbage cans and be kept moist. Don't make up huge amounts because it will break down and rot before you use it. The easiest way to mix the ingredients is to stir them together in a wheel barrow. Smaller amounts may be put in the garbage can and rolled around till mixed.

Of course, orchids can be grown in osmunda, straight tree fern, straight bark and gravel.

Osmunda comes in chunks of very wiry fibers. It used to be used extensively by commercial as well as private growers but is very difficult to use. It is hard to pot because all the fibers should run vertically and requires a good deal of pressing down with a potting stick. It stays quite moist, gives off some nutrients, but is terribly hard to remove when it is time to repot.

Tree fern is easy to pour in around the roots. Plants seem to "make roots" in tree fern. Often when you repot you discover that the roots are all around the pot and not in the mix. It washes out of the pot easily so water gently. Fertilizer with 18-18-18 when using tree fern alone.

Bark can be used alone. It seems to resist water at first and then gradually breaks down. During the breakdown process, nitrogen is used, therefore, one must fertilize with 30-10-10.

Whatever mix is used, it is a good idea to put new plants in your own mix. Repot as soon as possible depending upon the growth cycle of the plants. Paphs can be repotted even in bloom. Cattleyas never. Repot them when new growth has started and new roots are about one inch along. Then the plant will establish itself quickly.

Photo by Carl Webber

Cattleya mix—½ part fir bark, ¼ tree fern and ¼ part perlite

Photo by Carl Webber

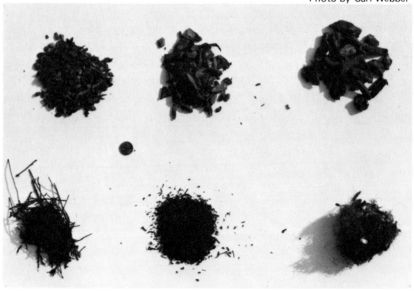

Top row, left to right—fine fir bark, medium fir bark, course fir bark. Bottom row—coarse tree fern, fine tree fern, redwood wool

If you purchase a plant, make sure the mix is in good condition. If it is spongy, soft or gooey, repot immediately.

Broken down mixes rot roots quickly, plants seem to wilt. There is no cure except repotting and waiting for the next growth cycle and the production of new roots.

TABLE 2
Do-It-Yourself Potting Mixes

Modified Off Mix	1/4th Size	Paph Mix	1/4th Size
3 gal. medium fir bark	3 qt.	4 gal. fine fir bark	1 gal. (4 qt.)
1 gal. medium redwood chips	1 qt.	1½ gal. coarse spaghnum	3 pt.
½ gal. peat lumps	1 pt.		
½ gal. coarse perlite	1 pt.	½ gal. med. redwood chips	1 pt.
¼ cup bone meal	1 tbs.	1 qt. hard limestone	1 cup
1 qt. hard limestone	1 cup	1/3 cup bone meal	1-1/3 tbs.
1 tbs. fritted potash	¾ tsp.	1 tbs. ground Dolomite	¾ tsp.
3 tbs. dried blood	2¼ tsp.		
1 tbs. ground Dolomite	¾ tsp.	3 tbs. dried blood	2¼ tsp.
4 cups water	1 cup	2 tbs. Superphosphate	1½ tsp.
		2 tbs. fritted potash	1½ tsp.
		(optional)	
		powdered limestone	1 cup
		sterilized, smashed gum balls	1 pt.
		sterilized, crushed oak leaves	1 cup

Cym Mix	1/4th Size	"Red Off"	1/4th Size
3 gal. medium redwood chips	3 qt.	5 gal. medium redwood chips	5 qt.
1 gal. fine peat	1 qt.	1 qt. hard limestone	1 cup
2 gal. peat lumps	2 qt.	2 qts. coarse Perlite	1 pt.
1 qt. hard limestone	1 cup	1 cup Bovung manure	4 tbs.
1/3 cup dried blood	1-1/3 tbs.	¼ cup bone meal	1 tbs.
¼ cup Superphosphate	1 tbs.	¼ cup gypsum	1 tbs.
¼ cup gypsum	1 tbs.	1 tbs. ground Dolomite	¾ tsp.
¼ cup ground Dolomite	1 tbs.		
1½ tbs. fritted potash	1-1/8 tsp.		
¼ cup bone meal	1 tbs.		

Courtesy of Delaware Orchid Society.

Pots

Many orchid growers are now using plastic pots. Plants stay wetter in plastic. The pots can be easily cut or drilled to make the drainage holes orchids love. Plastic pots are cheap and easy to clean, stack and store. They are, however, very light and easily tipped over if a big heavy cattleya is planted in them. It is also much more difficult to attach hangers and stakes. Paphs and Phalaenopsis really seem to do better in plastic pots. Many growers use plastic laundry baskets for big Cymbidiums.

Clay pots breathe. They also absorb salts from fertilizer. Algae grows on the outside. This makes them hard to clean. Since they are porous, plants dry out quicker. Any orchid that likes to dry out like Oncidiums or Dendrobiums do best in clay pots. Cattleyas, especially big growers, are easier to stake up.

Whatever type you choose, used pots must be cleaned. Bacterial, fungae and viral diseases can be passed on from dirty pots. A strong solution of chlorine in a bucket of water will sterilize pots. Use 1 cup of granular swimming pool chlorine (like HTH) to 3 gallons of water. Soak the pots for 24 hours. Remove pots and rinse copiously and let dry in the sun.

For the most part, orchids do better in shallow pots. If you already have deep pots, use extra crocking in the bottom. Some clay pots come with slits in the sides. These are great if you can get them. Lots of people enlarge the bottom drainage hole in clay pots by tapping carefully with a hammer and screw driver. If you do this, you must put ¼" wire screening over the hole to keep the mix from falling out. Do not use window screen. It is too fine and the bark dust may clog the drainage hole.

Fertilizers

As you noticed, some of the mixes include food for your orchids. Even so, growers using these mixes may wish to apply fertilizer.

Peters makes various formulations for orchids.

18-18-18 is used for plants in tree fern. Some growers use this during winter months.

30-10-10 is used for plants in bark or bark mixes.

Fish emulsion is a favorite food for orchids and is used instead of the others on a rotating basis.

Magamp is a sustained release fertilizer that is mixed in with the bark or tree fern mix.

Sustained release granules are used as well.

This group of products forms the backbone of a feeding program.

Pesticides

Here is a list of pesticides and fungicides to keep in your supply cabinet. This is a rapidly changing industry. Today new products are coming out in bewildering quantities and are being taken off the market as well. Here are some basics.

Malathion—emulsified concentrate or wettable powder. It smells terrible but is not very toxic. The concentrate sometimes causes damage to foliage or flowers and is quite hard on ferns. The wettable powder does not cause damage.

Kelthane is used for mites. Nothing else works as well.

Orthene is a new broad-spectrum bio-degradable systemic.

Whitmire prescription treatment no. 1200 is an aerosol synthetic pyrethroid for white fly control.

Natriphene S25 is a wettable powder equivalent of Zectran and is used as a dip to kill snails and slugs.

Fungicide Bactericides and Algecides

Physan general purpose fungicide bactericide and algicide. Excellent for seedlings out of flask. Good for soft rot on phalaenopsis.

Benomyl is a systemic fungicide.

Truban kills black rot and is good in combination with Benomyl.

Several words of warning are necessary at this point:

1. Read the labels.
2. Always store in original container.
3. Keep away from children and animals.
4. Do not use emulsified concentrate and wettable powder at same application.
5. Only make as much as you use in one application; do not store mixed insecticides.
6. Dispose of used containers carefully.

Stakes, Clips and Labels

You will need to use some method of keeping newly potted plants in the pots. Cattleyas and other tall plants may need staking.

ANYONE FOR ORCHIDS?

Hangers can be clipped onto the pots and the pseudobulbs wired to the hangers.

Pot clips or rhizome clips are another solution.

Plastic coated wire is used for wiring plants to hangers.

Nylon fishing line is most often used to "wire" plants to plaques.

Labels come in a variety of sizes and styles. There are labels printed with space for name, cross, award and flowering information. You can have your name printed on them. You can get them with wires or clips to put around the bulb. Most lables come with one side for pencil and one side for ink.

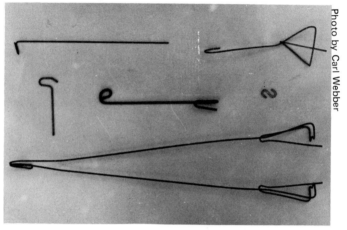

Top left—Phaph stake; top right—single pot hanger. Middle left—rhizome clip, stake and hook. Bottom—double pot hanger

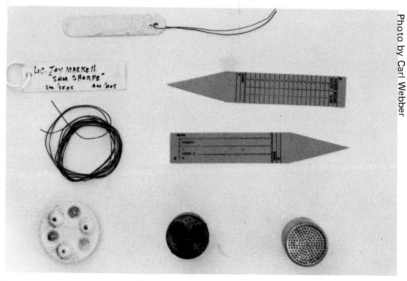

Labels, coated wire, drain, mister and rose

V

How to Place Your Plants in the Greenhouse

Arranging your plants in the greenhouse is like being married to a would-be decorator. She's forever moving the furniture. You're always moving your plants around. It's a terrible nuisance not to know where a certain plant is now. It's a mess if your plant blooms facing backward. There are some things you can do to make it better.

First of all, you should figure out your "micro-climates." Find your cool shady spots and your hot spots. Make a chart of the greenhouse showing the direction of the sun, drafty spots, heater, humidifier. Try to match your plants to better approximate their own native climate. Group all the Phalaenopsis in your warmest, shadiest spot. Find a cool moist shade area for the pleurothalids. Put your Dendrobiums in a high, dry sunny area. Try grouping all the miniatures in trays.

Perhaps your little plants on plaques would like to be suspended from the bottom of a big moss lined basket where your Stanhopea is growing. Eventually, you will find the perfect environmental niche for every plant. Make a diagram of it.

It is important that Cattleyas face the light properly. Put your label in the front of the pot near the front lead. Face the label and lead toward the light. This will make your plant bloom in the right direction. Do not change this orientation or your plant will grow toward the light and become misshapen.

Paphs also need to be oriented toward the light. In a fiberglass house, the light is less directional, so that the flower may face in any direction, but even so, if the plants are not moved, the stems will be straight.

A good greenhouse diagram might be set up like this. Bench areas will be labeled LB 1, LB 2, LB 3, RB 1, RB 2, RB 3. Under bench areas can be labeled LUB 1, LUB 2, LUB 3, RUB 1, RUB 2, RUB 3; hanging plants LH 1, LH 2, LH 3, etc.

69

```
                        1           1

              1         2           2         1

    1         2         3           3         2         1

    2         3        HR          HL         3         2
                    Hanging     Hanging
                      Left        Right
    3        LB                              RB         3
            Left                           Right
            Bench                          Bench
  ULB                                               URB
  Under                                            Under
  Left                                             Right
  Bench                                            Bench
```

Put this code on your label, then you will know where it goes when you have moved it for repotting or display.

Also, put this code in your record books. Then, any plant can be found with ease.

Another good idea is to color code your plants. Obtain some colored labels or even drink swizzle sticks in appropriate colors. Purple will be difficult, so leave it out. Any plant without a color code will be purple. All red plants will have a red tag, all white a white tag, all green a green tag, etc. Colored yarn can also be used but does fade after a while.

As an example of how critical the placement of certain plants can be, here is what happened to a plant of mine. A friend and I divided a blooming plant of *Oncidium* Kalihi. Her division continued to bloom. Mine sulked. I was chagrined. Everytime a new bud emerged from my spikes, it withered and dropped off. This sad state of affairs continued for three months. Finally, I moved my plant from the center of the bench to the front row, a matter of 10–12″. Its long spikes hung over into the aisle. Not an ideal place from my point of view, but the plant loved it. From that day on, it has never dropped another bud. I speculate that the greater air movement in the aisle is just what this little darling needed.

Every orchid grower has experiences like this. Keep trying until you have solved the puzzle. Orchids are really so hardy that they will hang in there until you do.

Stanhopea wardii 'Taylor El Toro' CCM/AOS—85 pts
Exhibited by Ronald Ciesinski
Short lasting, but fragrant and weird

One Kalihi 'Maryland' HCC/AOS
A Butterfly Orchid

Record Book

Don't think that you can get away without a record book. Naturally, you don't need to become obsessed with record keeping but the day may come when you can't remember the name or the parents of one of your hybrids.

There are excellent record books with printed blanks. You can use these or make your own. A small binder filled with blank file cards is perfect for a small hobby collection. It fits in a purse or pocket and can be taken along on a shopping spree.

Use one card for each hybrid plant. Write down the name of plant, award and year of award, if any. Put down the names of the cross and hybridizer. Include where it was purchased and the price. Later, if you plan to sell, trade or give a piece of it, put down the recipient. Write down a good description of the bloom; color of sepals and lip, general shape, etc. Plant Record Sheets can be purchased for 50/$4.95, 100/$9.50 plus 50¢ postage from Russells Greenhouse, 511 Ashby Drive, Charleston, Ill., 61920.

How to Place Your Plants in the Greenhouse

NAME _____ NO. _____

PARENTAGE _____

DATE ACQUIRED _____ SOURCE ____ PRICE _____

DESCRIPTION _____

CULTURE _____

DATE	BLOOM SPIKE	BLOOMS	REPOT	NOTES

Tricoglottis phillipinense var. braciata **A rarity and hard to bloom**

V I
Care of Plants

Watering

One of the great questions in all horticulture is how much to water, when to water and how often to water. No one ever tells you, because there really is no answer. Watering skills are learned by each person, sometimes, the hard way. Everyone has killed plants by over or under-watering. Here are a few hints that may help, but your plants will tell you if you make mistakes. Close observation of every plant will prevent deaths, but some deaths are inevitable even though orchids live very long lives.

First of all, never use water from a water softening system. Water from the municipal systems of large cities is satisfactory. If you are using well water, it should be tested for hardness. Hard water areas may have too many soluble salts. The following list shows whether your water is satisfactory for orchid cultures.

Less than 25×10^{-5} MHos = excellent
25–75×10^{-5} MHos = good
75–125×10^{-5} MHos = questionable
Over 125×10^{-5} MHos = unsatisfactory

If you have a problem, refer to the excellent article on page 39 of the American Orchid Society Handbook on Orchid Pests and Diseases.

Always water orchids in the morning. This gives your plants a chance to dry out during the day, so that water does not stand in the crowns of plants. When this happens, crown rot occurs. Wet plants and cool night temperatures are an invitation to fungus attack. Tepid water is best.

How much to water is rather tricky. Make sure that the orchid medium (tree fern mix or bark) is completely saturated. On big plants this means moving the hose to front, back and both sides. Water should pour out of the drainage holes. Smaller plants may be flooded without moving the hose nozzle around. Little plants and newly potted plants should be picked up and held in the palm of the hand trapping the water for a few seconds. The flow of water must be gentle enough not to dislodge the medium, but not so slow as to take all day. Some people attach a water breaker to their hose wand, others use the water on low volume straight from the wand.

How often watering is done is the $64,000 question. Experience is the answer, but here are some ideas. How often depends on temperature, how much light, how much humidity, how much air movement, and the time of year. The more light and air the plant is exposed to, the more often it needs watering. In low light and high humidity it will need less watering. On dark days in the winter, plants need less frequent watering. On hot summer days, outdoors in full sun, they will need watering daily. Small plants and miniatures dry out very fast and need more frequent watering than plants in big pots. Plants on plaques need to be sprayed every day.

As you progress into the more difficult to grow orchids, you will have to learn their specific watering needs. Place them in the greenhouse accordingly. For example, an area should be set aside for Dendrobiums that are resting. Newly potted Cattleyas should not be watered at all (only misted) until they start to grow and establish themselves.

Fertilizing

The application of fertilizer changes with the season. In northern climates in the last part of November, all of December and January and the first part of February, less fertilizer and water, for that matter, are needed.

During periods of vegetative growth, fertilizer applications can be stepped up. It does no good and considerable harm to fertilize a plant that is resting. This is where your powers of observation come in. Inspection is the ticket. Once a month pick up every plant (not Standard Cymbidium unless you like hernias) and look it over. Check for insect infestations while you're at it. When you see signs of new growth, you know the plant needs food. When that growth is completed and flowering is over, you know it needs a rest.

If all this fussing is not for you, there are other methods. In nature, after all, orchids receive dilute amounts of food everytime it rains, and you can do the same when you water. If you do this, dilute the fertilizer at least three times, i.e., 1 T per gallon becomes 1 t per gallon. I must warn you that occasionally you have to flush out the accumulated salts or too many salts will build up. When that happens, algae coats the outside of the pot, the mix has probably broken down and if left too long the roots will rot. Don't forget that in many tropical areas dry spells and rainy seasons occur. Even if you know where a plant comes from in nature and exactly what conditions it grows in all year round, it may need different care in a greenhouse.

Lots of growers set up a regular fertilizing program of fertilizing every other watering, willy nilly, and that may be the easiest if not the best.

What fertilizer you use depends on the orchid medium.

> Tree fern 18-18-18.
> Straight bark 30-10-10.
> Bark mixes, 30-10-10 or 18-18-18.

Fish emulsion should be used every third time just for a change of diet. Some growers use sustained release granules in which case they do not apply solutions of fertilizer when watering. If you go this route, take care. It is so easy to use too much. You will probably have to repot more often. Signs of overfertilization in Cattleyas, for instance, are blackened new growths.

Most Paph people use a mix incorporating all the nutrients needed, so of course, they don't add solutions of fertilizer when they water. Signs of overfertilization in Paphs are longitudinal grooves or ridges in the leaves and loss of roots.

PEST CONTROL

Inspection and a regular program are the answer to this problem. Everyone gets bugs, bush snails and slugs. But we don't have to keep them. Insect infestation not only disfigure and kill plants but can spread virus and bacterial infections from plant to plant.

Never forget that you must protect yourself, any pets and the environment from the toxic effects of pesticides.

The American Orchid Society has published an exhaustive treatise on the subject called Handbook on Orchid Pests and Diseases. Every orchid grower should own this book.

ANYONE FOR ORCHIDS?

Here are some useful ideas on how to set up a pest control program:

A. Set up a schedule on paper. Write down:
   1. Which chemicals
   2. How much
   3. How often
   4. Compatibility
B. Use protective gear—rubber gloves respirator, apron, and change clothes and bathe after application.
C. Make up only as much pesticide as needed for one application.
D. Do not store unused portion.
E. Store pesticides in original containers, never pop bottles or the like.
F. Dispose of used containers properly.

The National Agricultural Chemicals Association recommends:

QUICK, EASY RINSE & DRAIN PROCEDURE FOR PESTICIDE CONTAINERS

BEFORE USING ANY PESTICIDE
STOP
READ THE LABEL

1 Empty container into spray tank; drain in vertical position 30 sec.

2 Refill container 1/4-1/5 full; rinse thoroughly, pour into tank, drain.

3 Repeat rinsing & draining 3 times. Add fluid to bring tank up to level.

4 Crush container for recycling or burying. Drums can be reconditioned.

DO NOT REUSE CONTAINER! REDUCE HAZARDS!

Poster combines concise directions with attention-getting format.

Orchids are subject to the usual plant pests. Of course, careful inspection of each plant, cleanliness in the greenhouse, elimination of weeds near the foundation are the first steps in pest control. In a small greenhouse, it is possible to examine every plant once a month and nip pests in the bud. New plants should be isolated and treated before being brought in.

Once trouble is spotted, prompt action is required. Pests must be identified, the proper spray applied, with a follow-up spray to get the eggs.

Mites

Two spotted spider mites and false spider mites are very small and hard to see. Their damage, however, is quite apparent. The spider mites feed on the undersides of leaves producing a speckled appearance. Sometimes a very small webbing can be seen. False spider mites are even smaller, do not spin webs, and usually attack the surfaces of the leaves of phalaenopsis and other orchids. Their attack leaves pitting and silvering.

Two applications 7–10 days apart of Kelthane emulsified concentrate of 2 teaspoons per gallon of water will control spider mites.

Aphids

Aphids, often called plant lice, feed on buds and flowers. They secrete a honeydew which is so attractive to ants that they are "farmed" by ants. The honeydew also encourages fungus growth.

Thorough application of Malathion, 1 tablespoon per one gallon; repeat weekly if reinfestation appears or Orthene, 1 tablespoon per 1 gallon has systemic effect. Isotox or Meta Systox is also effective.

Mealybugs

Mealybugs are easy to spot. They are white insects with filaments. They lay their eggs in cottony sacs. The insecticide must actually touch them, so spray thoroughly.

Malathion—1 tablespoon per gallon, applied three times at three week intervals.

Orthene—1 tablespoon per gallon once a month has systemic action.

Scale Insects

Scale insects are quite common. There are both soft and hard or armoured scales The armoured kind have a hardened shield over their bodies. They congregate in hard-to-see places anywhere on the plant. Some eggs are not killed by sprays so careful follow-up action must be taken.

Malathion—2 tablespoons per gallon two or three times 7–10 days apart. Remove all papery coverings on Cattleyas because scale often hides under them.

White Fly

White fly used to be the bane of all greenhouse growers. They congregate on the undersides of host plants like fuchsias and fly all around if the plant is moved.

Whitemire prescription treatment no. 1200, aerosol generator. Use with a respirator according to directions on label.

Inspect all incoming plants for this pest; don't buy from greenhouses that have it; don't keep host plants like fuchsias, lantana, coleus and others.

Slugs and Bush Snails

Slugs have soft bodies and leave slimy trails. Bush snails are small, have a typical snail shell, and live in the bark mix. Bush snails are harder to eliminate than snails.

Ortho Slug-Geta containing Measurol. Use as a bait. Natriphene S25 is a highly effective wettable powder. Use it as a dip according to package instructions.

Snails like beer and can be drowned in shallow dishes of beer set around the greenhouse.

REPOTTING

The mechanics of repotting is really quite simple. When and how often is only a little more difficult.

Let us start first with seedlings. Use seedling grade tree fern or fir bark. I like one part tree fern, one part fir bark and half-part perlite for seedlings. Square plastic pots are ideal so that they can be grouped together in a plastic flat. Grouping helps you to keep track of them and they are not lost and shaded by mature plants.

Since seedlings are repotted so often, the mix they are in is probably not broken down. It's a great temptation to treat them like a fibrous rooted houseplant and just pot them without disturbing the root mass. This is not good practice. Remove the old mix as gently as possible and move the seedling into the next size pot. Make sure that it goes in at the same level as before and press the mix moderately firmly with your thumbs. Don't crush the roots but don't leave it so loose that the plant flops around.

Repotting Paphs

Paphiopedilums can be repotted any time of the growing cycle. They can be repotted while in bloom though I rather hate to do it then.

Here again, I use plastic pots but this time, round ones. The paphs look better in round pots and when on the bench, there is air space around them. Paphs are placed in the center of the pots and particular care is taken to make sure that the crown of the plant is right at "soil" level.

Remove all old medium, rinsing the plant in a solution of Benomyl 1 T per gallon. Examine the roots and remove old ones. New roots are plump and often times hairy. If the center of the plant is the oldest part and has died back, the plant may naturally fall into two pieces. If not, pot it as as. Hobby growers are better off with multiple growth plants. Naturally if the Paph is awarded or very valuable, you may wish to divide it and sell single growth divisions.

Making sure to keep the plant centered and at proper height, pack in the mix, working the mix in among the roots. Press down as you go. Pot firmly without crushing the roots. When you get done, the plant should not rock or flop and if there are lots of roots you should be able to pick up the plant pot and all by the foliage.

What to do if there are poor roots. Poor roots are withered and rotted. If this is the case, you had better check into your growing techniques. Overfertilizing paphs is a principle cause for root rot.

Paphs with no or poor roots are candidates for a live spaghnum moss nursery under lights. Follow the directions under flasks and put your labeled paph in such a unit. I recently ran an experiment with two almost rootless pieces of a valuable Paph; one piece had a new growth coming and enough root to be potted in the usual way. The other piece was totally rootless and was placed in a spaghnum unit. In a few months time it has far outstripped the other piece and has been potted up and put back in the greenhouse.

Paphs need to be repotted every year. Don't neglect them. If you have a small collection try to set aside a day or a week-end and do them all. You can set up an assembly line procedure. Do keep a record of when repotting was last done.

Repotting Phalaenopsis

Phalaenopsis can be scheduled for repotting every other year. Repot after the spring bloom is over. Most Phalies have lots of air roots coming out in all directions often very long roots at that. You'll have to use your judgment about what goes into the pot and what stays out.

Again, remove all the old mix and repot into round plastic pots. The crown should be in the center and slightly tipped off of vertical. This slanting of the plant in the pot lessens the chance of water collecting in the crown and causing crown rot. If you're a bossy, tidy person and can't stand all those surface roots, soak the roots in warm water to make them pliable. Then you can stuff them in the pot without snapping them off. You will try to make sure that the newly emerging roots are at "soil level."

At the time of repotting, you can cut back the old flower spike to three nodes. If the plant is good and strong, it will break a side shoot and continue blooming.

Repotting Miltonias

Miltonias love to be wet, but they also love good drainage. Here again, use plastic pots but snip out some extra drainage slits Put a layer of seedling grade mix on the bottom of your pot then add about an inch of fine aquarium gravel. Then pot the Miltonia in the center of the pot. One sure sign that your Miltonia is not getting enough water is pleated foliage. Repot when the new growth is about 2″ high. Avoid repotting during very hot summer weather. Leave enough room for two years growth but don't overpot.

Repotting Odontoglossums and Oncidiums

Again, repot every two years or if the plant is growing out of its pot. Remove old leafless bulbs and paint the wound with rose can sealer or dust with sulphur. Use medium grade mix. Place the oldest back part of the plant against the rim of the pot, thereby, leaving lots of room for new growths. I like clay pots for their quick drainage, and heavy stability. This is especially important if the plant is large or has a very big bloom spike. Repot when a new growth is about 2″ high.

Repotting Cymbidiums

Let's confine ourselves to Miniature Cymbidiums. Hobby growers with small greenhouses should not grow standards. You may be shocked to learn that many growers of standard cymbidiums for cut flowers throw away their plants when they get too big to divide.

Miniature Cymbidiums hate being disturbed, so plan on repotting on a three year basis. If yours is a young plant, remove the old mix with a hose and your fingers. Sometimes there is not much else but roots in the pot. However, near the center there is usually some old bark. Use a lot of crocking in the bottom of a standard height clay pot. Remove any old leafless bulbs and repot using cymbidium mix medium grade. Use a stick to work the mix in and around the roots and pot firmly.

If the plant needs dividing you will need a cleaver and hammer to get the plant apart. Divide it into three or four growth plants. Make your cut so that the newest growths make up the new plant. Remove old back bulbs. If the plant is valuable, you can save the back bulbs for propagating. Don't forget to leave enough room for three years growth.

Repotting Cattleyas

Nothing is more unattractive than a neglected cattleya plant. The vegetative parts are basically not that beautiful, and when they have grown over the edge of the pot and fasten their roots to the outside of the pot, they are really a horror. Lots of growers put cattleyas on a two-year schedule. I advise repotting when they need it. So much depends on the growth habit of the plant that you can't always go by a schedule.

Cattleya overdue for repotting; new roots will be damaged

Cattleya—ready for repotting

If the next new lead hangs over the edge of the pot, it's time for action. Wait until the new growth is starting and is about 1 or 2″ long. If you wait longer and new roots are emerging, they will be damaged in handling. If the plant is to be divided, decide where, and cut through the rhizome with a sterilized knife before you remove the plant from the pot. Cutting afterwards subjects the plant to too much manhandling. Remove all old medium, washing it off in a bucket of water if necessary.

Position the plant in an azalea clay pot with the back portion right up against the back edge of the pot. Make sure the new growth is level. Never let it tip up so that the new growth grows up in the air.

I do not remove old roots unless there are lots of them. Long live roots can be trimmed but leave 5 or 6″ at least. Pot using medium grade mix, pressing down as you go and working in the medium with your fingers. Don't crush and jam but make it good and firm.

Cattleyas usually need to be staked up. This is easy in clay pots because you can fasten a rhizome clip or a stake to the rim of the pot. A big, heavy plant will need both clip and stake. Position the stake right behind the back bulb. Using plastic coated "telephone" wire stakes as follows:

Wrap the wire around the stake leaving two equal ends. Make a loop around the bulb, twist it until you get to the next bulb, twist again, etc. Make sure you have enough wire left to include the new growth when it has matured. Don't loop tightly or you may strangle the plant.

If the cattleya is to hang, put the hanger on the sides of the plant so that the new growth is not going toward the hanger. Don't wire to the hanger. It's too much work to remove the hanger if you decide to bench the plant later.

Repotting Cane Dendrobiums

Repot Dendrobiums when they are overcrowded or growing over the edge of the pot. The best time is when the new growth is 3 or 4″ high and new roots are forming. Remove the old back bulbs, put the plant in the smallest pot that will allow two new growths. Do not overpot. Often the plant will be top heavy with such tall bulbs and such a tiny pot. Either hang the plant or place it on the bench in a clay pot one size bigger than the pot it is planted in. This will prevent tipping it over.

HINTS AND ADVICE

A few other remarks need to be made about plant care. If you cut any part of any plant, you must sterilize the knife before you go on to the next plant. If you do not take this precaution, you very well may spread incurable virus from one plant to the next. Sterilize your knife or clipper with the flame from a laboratory alcohol burner, Benzene torch or a candle flame.

Make sure to pick off old flowers and dead leaves as they accumulate. The old flower stalks and sheaths should be clipped off neatly near the leaf.

Remove the papery covers of cattleya bulbs to prevent hidden bug infestations.

Keep an eye open for flower spikes and be prepared to stake or train them as needed.

If a plant sticks in the pot, run a knife around the pot. If that fails, soak the plant in a bucket of warm water until it loosens. Naturally, if you are dealing with a badly overgrown cattleya or cymbidium you may not be able to cut around the pot, or get it into a bucket without damaging the plant. So, if all else fails, break the pot.

Staking Bloom Spikes

Odontoglossum and allied intergeneries need to have their bloom spikes trained. Wait until the lower part of the spike is 14–17" long. Test to see if the lower portion is stiff. If so, you may insert a stiff wire. If you want a curved bloom spike, bend your wire to the desired curve. Start tying with raffia and continue to tie as the spike stiffens. Usually the end of the spike is allowed to droop freely giving a gracefulness to the display. Naturally, you can also train the spike to be straight by following the same procedure.

Oncidiums with 6' bloom spikes can be trained in much the same way. They can be trained into a circle but you must not wait till the spike is too stiff to bend.

Phalaenopsis spikes can be supported from the ceiling or sides of the greenhouse by a gadget called a Nie-Co-Rol. This is a reel device with a plastic hook that will hold a phalaenopsis spike in a graceful arch. If you wish to transport your phalaenopsis to the show table, you had better stake them as described above.

The stake should be long enough to support the lower portion of the spike letting the flowers droop into a pleasing arch.

Staking Paphiopedilums is an art, neglected by some, but when done well, makes a superb presentation. Paphs tend to lean forward. They need to be staked before the flower is "set." Cut a stake no longer than one-quarter of the way up the dorsal sepal. Place the stake as close to the stem as possible. Tie with raffia or green string just below the ovary, encircling the stake and stem. A second tie may be made almost at the center of the flower. If this staking is done too late, the flower will "look at the sky" instead of the viewer.

Another method to support a Paph flower is to shape a wire into a hook and bend it at right angles. This wire should be inserted near the plant. The stem rests in the crook of the hook. You can make up several of these in different lengths and keep them on hand.

HOW TO "TREE UP THE RIGHT BARK"

Epiphytic means growing in air. Lots of orchids grow in nature perched in the tops of trees with their roots free and ready to absorb the nutrients they need from the air, dew, mists and rain. Some epiphytes object to life in a flower pot. Some have pendulous blooms. If you want to keep the former happy and be able to see the blooms on the latter, you've got to "bark" them.

Materials available to mount orchids on are pretty varied:

Tree fern slabs or sticks or balls.
Cork bark.
Smooth cork slabs.
Cedar shingles.
Sassafras branches or twigs.
Lilac branches.
Manzita burls.
Driftwood.

One cardinal rule in mounting plants is to try to do it at the beginning of a growth cycle. That way, the plant will establish itself quickly. Newly mounted plants should not be put in an exposed or sunny spot. Even if they ordinarily like lots of light, don't move them into such a spot until their roots have grown into the mounting material.

Oncidium mounted on tree fern plaque

Equitant Oncidium mounted on cork slab

Equitant Oncidium mounted vertically on sassafras twig

Photo by Carl Webber

Photo by Carl Webber

Equitant Oncidium mounted on cedar shingle

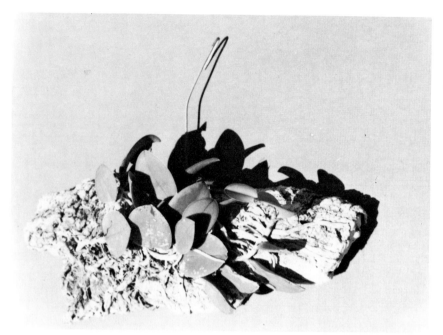

Miniature orchid mounted on cork bark

Miniature orchid mounted on twig swing

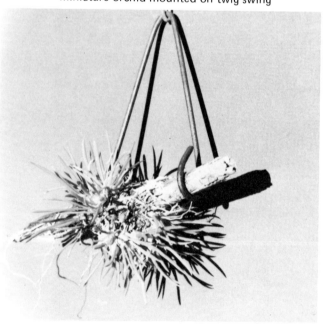

One often forgotten rule of horticulture is that you are trying to make plants grow and thrive and *then* bloom. Let your plants get a good start. Sometimes a weak plant blooms in one final attempt to reproduce itself and promptly croaks.

Well now, how do you mount your plant? Some people prefer to put a small wad of osmunda or spaghnum moss between the plant and the plaque. Others tell you that simply delays the attachment of the plant to the plaque. I guess it depends whether the plant wants to be moist and whether you've a dryish greenhouse or a wettish one.

Here you are with your plant, your plaque and your pad, if any. What to tie it with? Plastic coated telephone wire is unsightly but easy. It doesn't rot and it doesn't cut into the plant. It can be removed after the plant is established. Monofilament fishing line or plastic sewing thread is inconspicuous, won't rot, but is hard to tie, and may cut into the plant.

Whichever you use, tie it tightly. If you don't, the newly emerging roots will be damaged by rubbing against the plaque everytime the plant is touched or watered.

Another method is to staple a strip of plastic wire screening around the plant and plaque. It works but it is awfully ugly until you get the plant established.

Here is a short, partial list that at least indicates the wide variety of plants that like to be mounted—not potted.

Aerangis biloba
Aerangis rhodosticta
Angraecum distichum
Angraecum eichlerianum
Brassavola cuculata
Brassavola perrinii
Broughtonia sanquinea
Cattleya aclandiae
Cattleya luteola
Cirrhopetalum species
Dendrobium aggreagatum
Dendrobium linguiforme
Dendrobium pierardii
Dendrobium primulinum
Dendrochilum filiforme
Epidendrum polybulbon

91

ANYONE FOR ORCHIDS?

Epidendrum porpax
Eria fragrans
Gastrochilus species
Haraela odorata
Leptotes bicolor
Leptotes unicolor
Maxillaria species
Nageliella (Hartwegia) purpurea
Oncidium (equitant types)
Oncidium cebolleta
Oncidium jonesianum
Oncidium teres
Ornithocephalus species
Polyrrhiza funalis
Renanthera species
Rodriguesia species
Sophronitis species
Stenia pallida
Tricoglottis philippinense
Vanda hookeriana

The mechanics of attaching hardware to the plaques is rather easily solved. It is easy enough to push wire through tree fern plaques and then bend the wire into a loop or a hook. If the wire is stiff, use two pliers to bend it. Otherwise, the force may splinter the plaque. Of course, if the plaque is heavy and dense, it may be necessary to predrill the hole.

I find that cork bark, being somewhat thicker, needs to be drilled. Another method is to drive a nail through, pull it out, and put in your hook.

Sassafras branches, having rough bark that doesn't come off as it ages, are ideal for mounting purposes. If you saw the branch slightly on the diagonal, water will not collect on the top. You can paint the top cut with a clear plastic coating to keep it from rotting. Drill a hole in the center, and screw in an eye or a cup hook, and you're in business.

Twigs can be handled in several ways. You can make a little harness of wire to hold the twig horizontal, something like a swing. You can let them hang vertically from a bit of nylon fishing line tied on.

One of the most attractive ways to use twigs takes a little more doing, but is well worth the effort. If you have arty, crafty kids, they may love this project.

Get the following supplies:

A muffin tin
Paper muffin cups
A small amount of cement
Your twigs

Put a paper muffin cup into as many holes in the muffin tin as you wish. Make up cement according to the directions on the package. Pour the cement into the prepared cups. When it has set sufficiently to hold the twigs upright, place the twigs in the center. Try to use branched or interestingly shaped twigs. When set, remove the paper, and you have a solid little tree that can sit on the bench or a shelf, and make an attractive home for any number of mini-orchids. This same technique can be used to make a "tree" big enough to hold several orchids and bromiliads. Just use a big branch and a coffee can for the cement form.

Stakes and Hangers

Using a wire bender, jigs and pliers you can make your own stakes and hangers.

Wire former can be purchased from the Freshes, 8777 S.W. 76th Street, Miami, Fla. 33143 for $6.98 and $.61 postage. It comes complete with instructions for making rhizome clips, ring hangers, stakes, etc.

The following instructions may help:

WIRE BENDING FOR BEGINNING ORCHID GROWERS

Stake for 6" Pot
Cut #9 wire 18" long.
First bend, 2¼" from right end to center pin, clockwise 180°.
Third bend 2", clockwise.
Fourth bend 2", counterclockwise.
Height above pot rim 7¾".
For other heights, add 10¼" for bends to the desired height.
For other pot sizes, add 7¼" to one-half pot size + desired height.

ANYONE FOR ORCHIDS?

Hanger for 4" Pot (also 3" and light 5")
   Cut #12 wire 30" long.
   First bend 7" from right end to center pin, clockwise 90°.
   Second bend 3½" from first bend, clockwise 90°.
   Third bend close, ends held vertically, 90° clockwise.
   Fourth bend close, ends held vertically, 90° counterclockwise,
      90°.
   Fifth bend, wires still vertical, 1-3/8", clockwise, about 15°.
   Sixth and seventh bends bringing ends together to form equi-
      lateral triangle.
   Eighth bend 3-1/8" from base of triangle, counterclockwise,
      30°.
   Final bends in vice, and around big pin to form hook.
   Height about 15" above pot rim.
   For other heights, add 15" for bends to the desired height
      above pot.

Hanger for 5" Pot (also 4" and 6")
   Cut #9 wire 36" long.
   First bend 8" from right end, clockwise 90°.
   Second bend 4" from first bend, clockwise 90°.
   Third bend close, ends held vertically, clockwise 90°.
   Fourth bend close, ends held vertically, counterclockwise 90°.
   Fifth bend, wires still held vertically, 2-3/8", about 10°,
      clockwise.
   Sixth bend, wires still held vertically, 7/8", about 10°, clock-
      wise.
   Seventh and eighth bends crossing ends to form equilateral
      triangle.
   Ninth bend 3½" from base of triangle, counterclockwise 30°.
   Final bends in vice, and around big pin to form hook.
   Height about 20" above pot rim.
   For other heights, add about 16" for bends to the desired
      height above pot.

Courtesy Southeastern Pennsylvania Orchid Society, Inc.

Ansellia Africana var. 'Verapaz' AM/AOS—81 pts
Exhibited by May & Craig Orchids
Easy summer bloomer

94

Photo by John C. Krauer, M.D.

SUMMERING

Even orchids need a summer vacation. For many plants, this is the prime growing time. They benefit from fresh air and sunshine just like their owners do. But plants outside can not only get sunburned but even buggy.

If you grow your plants on a window sill and have a terrace or porch you can treat your plants to an excellent vacation. The ideal conditions for orchids is a spot that gets early morning sun, mid-day shade and plenty of air movement. If this can be accomplished with exposure to rain as well, so much the better.

Hanging plants from protecting fences (like basket weave) or from open trees is ideal. This method simulates the natural habitat of many orchids.

Lots of growers construct lath houses and shelters. Plans can be found in many magazines, and garden construction books at your local building supplier.

Simple racks can be constructed from 2 X 4s and galvanized pipe in sawhorse style.

A summer lath shelter—very easy to make

A marvelous summer shelter for orchids and people

Wire screening can be attached around the circumference of a tree and small plants hooked on. Watch out for squirrels.

Fancy plant stands are swell for Paphs and Phalaenopsis if you don't have too many of them. Just make sure the stands are in a very sheltered spot and not close to a brightly reflective wall.

Even if the plants are watered by summer rains, care must be taken during dry spells. Plants in a great deal of light outdoors transpire a lot and must have generous watering. Small plants, especially, dry out very fast and will need watering every sunny dry day.

Plants get acclimatized to their environment and resent abrupt changes so beware of moving a plant directly to a very different spot. For example, cymbidiums like full summer sun but will burn if moved from the shelter of a greenhouse to a patio or deck. Move them gradually into more and more light.

Never put orchid plants directly in the ground for the summer. Don't put plants on the ground. They still need perfect drainage and air circulation.

Greenhouse shaded by slats

Summer outdoor care is tricky so daily inspection is necessary. Don't think you can just put them out like the cat and forget them.

During the outdoor growing season, plants will need plenty of fertilizing. Now is a good time for fish emulsion or manure tea. Just don't use them right before a garden party.

Manure tea is made by placing two cups of Bovung dried cow manure in a cheesecloth bag. (I use the sleeve from an old shirt tied at each end.) Suspending the bag in a garbage can of water, put on the cover and let it "work" for about 2 weeks. It smells foul but the orchids love it.

During this growing period, use a fertilizer high in nitrogen even if you grow in tree fern like Peters 30-10-10. This will stimulate strong new growth.

Some growers especially Cymbidium growers apply 10-30-20 a few times after the new growths are made up to stimulate bloom production.

Remember not to overfertilize. Water the plants with plain water to flush any excess salts every third or fourth watering.

Plants hanging outside don't suffer from insect infestation because of the good air circulation and copious water. They don't seem to infect each other like they do in greenhouses. However, don't fall into complacency. Do inspect them and take steps if needed.

Lath shelter next to fiberglass house

Photo by Carl Webber

Plants outside on benches are more at risk and any plant on a deck or patio floor is easy prey to slugs and bush snails. Sharp sand spread under the bench area discourages slugs.

When to bring in the plants depends on which genera and your climate. Warm growers should be brought in when the nights fall regularly into the upper fifties. Remember that most of them need some cool nights to trigger bloom. Intermediates can stay out until it gets to the lower fifties but not too long. Leave the cool growers out as long as possible even if you are growing on a window sill, leave them out. They will benefit more from the cool treatment than from the avoidance of shock. I bring my Cymbidiums in on any night that gets close to 32° and I watch the thermostat like a hawk. In fact, I carry them in and out several times during the late fall.

To prevent bringing in any insects on your summered plants, you must dip them in a Malathion bath unless you have carried out an extensive pesticide program all summer with a systemic. Even so, most growers dip their plants. This dipping prevents bugs from coming in inside the pots. Be sure to wear rubber gloves during this operation, and let the plants drain before bringing them in after the dipping.

V I I
Growing Young Plants

SEEDLINGS

Sooner or later, seedlings, community pots, flasks and hybridization will enter the picture.

Seedlings should be unbloomed so that you get just as much chance at an award winner as the grower. Seedlings come in all sizes ranging from "dug ups" from community pots to big plants ready to bloom. Lots of Phalaenopsis growers sell them by the inch measured from the tip of the left leaf to the tip of the right. In many ways, it is the most fair way, because it's hard to tell how big a plant is from the pot size listed in a catalogue.

In any case, when your seedlings arrive, it's a good idea to re-pot them in your own mix. Some of them will come "bare root," that is unpotted. Pot them in a pot appropriate for one year's growth. Overpotting or two year potting is hard on seedlings. After all, if you are going to the trouble of raising "babies" you want to give them lots of tender loving care.

Treat them as you would any newly potted plant, misting often. Put them in a rather sheltered spot until you can see that they are coming along.

Seedlings need to have the best conditions you can give them. When they are established, put them in a warm and sunny place where they are in plain view. Inspect them weekly, at least.

Water them more frequently than your big plants, and water gently. A balanced fertilizer in every dilute solution keeps them moving right along. If you employ a scheduled preventative pesticide program, be careful. They are far more sensitive to toxic effects from pesticides than mature plants.

Phalaenopsis seedlings are subject to rot if the conditions are not right, i.e., too much humidity and cool temperatures. If this happens, keep them drier (mist only on sunny days) and move them to a warmer spot. Treat them with Physan (1 T to a gallon of water). This works like a charm on Phalaenopsis soft rot.

Nothing quite takes the place of watching the flower development of a first blooming seedling. It starts with seeing those proto-buds down deep in the sheath growing, pushing their way out. Now you can see how many buds and start guessing about the color. Finally, the bud droops its head and starts to open. When the flower is fully open, make a record of the date, number of flowers, color of sepals and lip, carriage of spike and any other information. If it changes color as the flower ages, record that too. Take a good color slide.

Community Pots

Now that you can handle seedlings, graduate to communities. These little guys are small and like the comfort of their fellows. They may be shipped in the community. If so, leave them be. Until they are really crowding each other and ready for 2 inch pots, they are better off together. Put them near your seedlings and keep an eye on them. Slugs just love tender young things and can mow down a whole pot in one night. Lots of snail bait, saucers of beer and eternal vigilance is the ticket.

Community pot of Cattleya alliance seedlings   Photo by Carl Webber

Photo by Carl Webber

Community pot of equitant *Oncidiums* in gravel mulch

If the communities come bare root, you have a tricky job. Group them (approximately 5-8) in a 4 inch bulb pan. Use very fine bark mix or very fine tree fern. Tree fern is the easiest because it seems to pour right in and all around. Make sure the seedlings get in deep enough. They seem to work their way out thereby exposing tender roots. A top dressing of very fine gravel will hold them down.

When the time comes to move the youngsters from community to individual pots, you will discover a tangle of roots. To get them apart without damage, dip them in a bowl of luke-warm water. Let them soak just a few minutes and, lo and behold, they slip apart without trouble. Pot them up, label and put them with your other seedlings.

Flasks

Now you are ready for the "big time"—flasks. What are you going to do with all those plants of the same cross? Simple. Go in with some friends. Each one pays his share and grows on his own babies. Make a pact that if anyone wins an award, the others will get vegetative divisions first. Then you can have it meristemmed.

If one of the group is an especially good grower, let him keep all the flasklings for the first month. This is the most critical time.

Paphiopedlium seedlings in a flask

Paphiopedilums in a flask

How big the plants are in a flask varies. Some are so big that you must break the bottle to get them out. A few may be big enough for 2 inch pots. Sometimes equitant oncidiums are in bloom in the flask. The bigger, the better, with flasks.

When the flask arrives, inspect it carefully. If it has gotten too hot, liquid may have oozed from agar and the plants may have cooked. The agar may have broken up. These need attention right away. If the agar is in good shape and the seedlings small, put them under your lights and grow them on a bit.

To remove the plants is really not hard. Wash out your sink and rinse well. Moisten paper towels and put them on the drainboard. Run the water and regulate the temperature to blood warm. Fill a big bowl with this warm water, add a small amount of Physan. Keep the water running in the sink. Open the lid, run in some tap water, agitate gently, and wash out some seedlings into the bowl. If the plants are small, they will float right out. If the agar is hard, they may stick. Just be patient and gentle and eventually they will all be washed out. Of course, if the plants are really big, you should break the bottle with a tap from a hammer.

Wash off all the agar and sort the plants by size on to the towels. If there are really big ones, they can be treated like seedlings. The next biggest can be put in communities. The smallest should go into live spaghnum moss and put under fluorescent lights.

Here's how to set up spaghnum moss nurseries for your flasklings. Get some plastic sweater boxes, drill holes for drainage if you like. You don't need the holes if you are very vigilant. The flasklings must not dry out or swim. Put in a layer of pea gravel, next a layer of pine needles, over this live spaghnum moss collected from the woods if you can get it or long fibered moss sold in a plastic bag. Dibble in the seedlings in rows in the moss, cover with the lid and put under the lights. This treatment is perfect for flasklings one-quarter inch to one inch size.

Do not use any pesticides or chemicals in the spaghnum boxes or the spaghnum will die. Water only with chlorine free water. You can accomplish this by letting water stand in a wide mouthed container over night. It is permissible to fertilize these units with very dilute 18-18-18. Overfertilization and too much light will encourage the growth of algae on the spaghnum with disastrous results. This method of getting flasklings started will save lots of the smaller fellows, but do move them on into communities as soon as you can.

When they are big enough for communities, pot them as described above and distribute among your "combine."

Some growers put their flasklings into plastic market packs instead of bulb pans. Often they cover them with propped up newspaper for a week to protect them from loss of humidity and from overexposure to the sun.

The greatest dangers to flasklings are too much light, too much or little water, slugs and fungus. Drench fungused plants with Physan. If that doesn't help, try Natriphene.

Be resigned that you will lose some flasklings but try it anyway and fight hard to save them. The rewards are great.

HYBRIDIZATION

Perhaps hybridization is not too practical for the hobby grower, but there are some good reasons for trying it.

First of all, if you own fine varieties of species plants, selfing them or sibling crossing them is a service to horticulture. Today, with strict laws for the protection of native orchids, selfing and sibling crosses are one way of making sure that species plants survive. If you do wish to help in this way, send your pod to a grower or dealer who specializes in species plants. He will be glad to grow them on for distribution and sale to other hobbyists and will probably trade you a seedling or something you don't own.

Second, if you own good awarded stock and really know something about the trends in breeding, you can make good hybrids.

Third, you can add to the common knowledge by trying some intergenerics. This is a complex subject so don't try it unless you understand something of compatibilities and have knowledge of what has been done and what works. Keep meticulous records and try to correspond with someone else in the field. Be prepared for many disappointments.

Here is a thumbnail sketch of the mechanics of breeding an orchid.

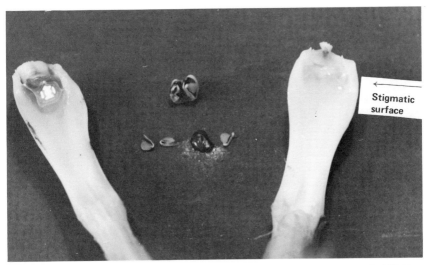

Photo by Carl Webber

Left: Cattleya column intact. Upper middle: anther cap.
Lower middle: anther cap and pollinea. Right: column
anther cap removed (stigmatic surface)

Cattleya seed pod   Photo by Carl Webber

107

Center: split seed pod with millions on minute seed. Right:
seed pod prior to taking out seed which is then sterilized
and sown on the sterile agar medium in the flasks

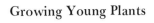

Paphiopedilum Silver Anniversary

Slc. Petite's Wink
Jones and Scully, Inc.

aeliocattleya persepolis 'Spendor' AM/AOS
Armacost & Royston, Inc.

Paphiopedilum Freckles 'Bright Eyes'
AM/AOS   Hanes Orchids

Doritaenopsis mem. Maggie Fields 'Malibu'
HCC/AOS   Arthur Freed Orchids Inc.

Orchids growing in test tubes

The pollen is attached to the column by a viscid disk and a little strip called a stipe. They are protected by an anther cap. You must remove the anther cap to get at the pollen. Sometimes the pollen comes off with the cap. Sometimes it falls out so be prepared when you remove the anther cap with a pair of tweezers. Place a card or piece of paper under the column to catch the pollen.

Next, you touch the stigmatic surface which is quite sticky with a pointed stick. Pick up the pollen and it will adhere to this sticky fluid. Press the pollen on the stigmatic surface. And the job is done. The first sign of success is the wilting of the flower and the thickening of the ovary.

Make a tag and tie it on the ovary. The tag should name the cross and the date of pollinization and a code number. You may not wish to tell the person who flasks your seed the name of your cross; therefore, the code number.

One last contribution in the field of hybridizing is to form a pollen bank. If you are friendly with a local commercial grower and hybridizer, he will be only too glad to trade pollen from awarded or rare plants for community pots or seedlings.

Here is a description of how to store pollen until the right plant comes into bloom.

In an old pill bottle or a test tube, place a small amount of calcium hyperchloride (available in any drug store). Cover the chemical with some crumpled paper. This is to insure that the pollen doesn't touch the chemical desicant. Touch the end of a toothpick to the stigmatic surface. Then, pick up the pollen with the sticky toothpick. The pollen will adhere. Put pick, pollen and all in the tube and cover. Tape the label on the outside and store in the refrigerator. It will keep six months or so, until you are ready to use it.

How long to leave on the pod depends upon not only the genera but on other factors such as environmental conditions. A good many laboratories prefer to have you send the pod while still green. In most cases, the longer a seed pod stays on the plant, the better. If the pod contains no viable seed, it will yellow and drop off. It if is left on too long, it will dehisce (split open) and the seed will be dissipated.

Seed Pod Harvesting Schedule

Brassavola nodosa and other terete brassavolas	4–5 months
Brassavola digbyana and gauca	5–6 months
Cattleya hybrids (labiata)	4–5 months
Cattleya hybrids (bifoliate)	4–5 months
Epicattleya	5 months
Epidendrum	4–5 months
Laelia hybrids	4–5 months
Schomburgkia hybrid	4–5 months
Broughtonia hybrids	60 days
Oncidium triquetrum hybrids	5 months
Oncidium equitant (other)	60 days
Oncidium papilio	100 days
Oncidium kramerianum	100 days
Oncidium limminghei	100 days
Oncidium spacelatum types	4 months
Onc luridum type	6–8 months
Miltonia hybrids	4 months
Odontoglossum hybrids	5–7 months
Ascocenda and Vanda	5–7 months
Rhynchostylis hybrids	5–8 months
Dendrobium phalaenopsis	4–5 months
Dendrobium nobile	5 months
Dendrobium pierardii types	6–7 months
Phalaenopsis hybrids	110 days

Orchids naturalized out of doors in California

Broughtonia sanguinea 'Mission Chimes' AM/AOS

VIII
What's in a Name?

NOMENCLATURE

An orchid by any other name . . . remains the same beautiful plant but in the world of serious growers and botanists, the correctness of the name is of crucial importance. As you will see, the system used for naming orchids is completely systematic, which makes it easy to follow when one has learned the system.

I have now written here a comprehensive account of how orchids are named. Anyone wishing to read such an account can refer to "Handbook of Orchid Nomenclature and Registration," Second Edition, published by the International Orchid Commission. My account is, rather, an explanatory general introduction to the subject. After reading it, you should have a clear picture of the basic issues. Hopefully, you will be able to find your way around and avoid the more obvious kinds of errors.

The accompanying diagram shows how the entire Plant Kingdom is broken down into categories and sub-categories. For all practical purposes, you only need to know that all orchids are members of the Class Angiosperms, Family *Orchidaceae*.

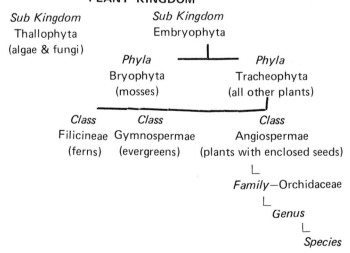

PLANT KINGDOM

Sub Kingdom
Thallophyta
(algae & fungi)

Sub Kingdom
Embryophyta

Phyla ——————— *Phyla*
Bryophyta   Tracheophyta
(mosses)   (all other plants)

Class   *Class*   *Class*
Filicineae Gymnospermae   Angiospermae
(ferns)   (evergreens)   (plants with enclosed seeds)

L

Family—Orchidaceae

L

Genus

L

Species

115

GETTING THE MESSAGE FROM YOUR LABELS

Let's give you a few examples of what your orchid label is trying to tell you.

If the plant is a species the label will read like this:

Brassavola nodosa

This means that you have a plant from the genus Brassavola, and that the particular species is nodosa.

If the plant is a hybrid, the label may say:

Lc. Bonanza 'Paydirt' AM/AOS

This means that you are not only lucky, but have a Laelia-cattleya named Bonanza. It is a division or a meristem of one particular Bonanza. (There may be many thousands of other Bonanzas.) Your particular Bonanza was shown for an award before AOS judges and received an Award of Merit (AM). At this time it was given the variety name 'Pay Dirt.' All divisions and meristems of that plant are called Bonanza 'Pay Dirt' and carry the award.

Suppose that your label says:

Lc. Bonanza X Blc. Norman's Bay

This means that your plant's mother is Laeliacattleya Bonanza and its father is Brassolaeliacattleya Norman's Bay. When the breeder of this plant bloomed the first seedling, he applied for a name for this seedling. He named it and registered it as:

Blc. Memoria Crispin Rosales

All the thousands of seedlings from that original breeding and those from any subsequent breeding having those two parents must be called Blc. Memoria Crispin Rosales. Therefore, your your label can say on one side:

Blc. Memoria Crispin Rosales

And on the other side it can say:

Lc. Bonanza X Norman's Bay

If the Bonanza and the Norman's Bay used in the breeding were awarded, the label could read, for example:

Lc. Bonanza 'Pay Dirt' AM/AOS
X
Blc. Norman's Bay 'Gothic' AM/AOS

If you buy flasks and seedlings, you may be buying plants that have not yet been named. Until they have been named by the hybridizer, they are called by their parented name with the X in between. The Royal Horticultural Society publishes a list of all the orchid hybrids. You can look up the name of one parent and find the reference to the other parent and the new name.

System of Nomenclature

Before we investigate the system of the naming of orchids a few definitions are in order.

Genus: plural, genera, a subdivision of a family, consisting of one or more species which show similar characteristics and appear to have a common ancestry.

Species (singular and plural): a group of plants showing intergradation among its individuals and having in common one or more characteristics which definitely separate it from any other group; a kind of plant distinct from other kinds.

Naming of orchids seems to be a complicated business. Actually, plant nomenclature follows very strict rules.

1. The specific name of an orchid species consists of two terms in Latin form.
    a. The first term is the generic name telling the name of the genus to which the plant belongs, i.e., Cattleya, Phalaenopsis, Cymbidium.
    b. The second term is the specific epithet telling the species of the genus to which the plant belongs.

These two words together give you the name of the species or the specific name. The first term is always capitalized, the second, even though named after a person, is not. When printed, they both should be italicized.

Example: *Cattleya skinneri.*

Often a wild plant will be given a varietal name to designate it from others in the species. This is a botanical variety and is given a varietal epithet. It is expressed in italics and preceded by the abbreviation for variety (var.). When printed, the Genus, species and varietal epithet are italicized, the word "var." is in lower case and not italicized.

Example: *Cymbidium lowianium* var. *concolor.*

Cultivated plants are given a cultivar epithet. This name

117

should be a fancy name (not Latinized) and in Roman print. It must be enclosed by single quotation marks.

Example: *Cymbidium lowianium* var. *concolor* 'Picardy.'

2. The specific name of an orchid hybrid also has two names.
    a. The first term is the generic name or a new hybrid-generic name.
3. The second term is called a grex epithet. It must be a fancy name (not Latinized) and both capitalized and printed in Roman type.

Hybrid plants can also be given cultivar names in which case the cultivar name is expressed in single quotes, Roman type and a fancy name.

Example: Cattleya Bob Betts 'Goliath,' Laeliacattleya Culminant 'La Tuillieies' Asconopsis Irene Dobkin 'Orange Delight.'

In horticulture practice, until a new hybrid has been named and registered by its hybridizer, it is known by its parent's names and a multiplication sign meaning cross.

Example: *Epidendrum tampense* × *plicatum* after registration by W. W. G. Moir becomes Epidendrum Grand Bahama.

Once a particular cross has been registered and named, that name must be applied to this cross even though it is "remade" later.

A cultivar name continues to be used on any vegetative division including meristems.

Hybrid generic names are often a combination of the different generic names of each plant.

For example: Cattleya_____ × Laelia _____ = Laeliocattleya_____ .

The list on pages 119–150 will give you all the presently acceptable names for genera and hybrids involving two or more genera.

Courtesy of International Orchid Commission from Handbook on Orchid Nomenclature and Registration.

ACAMPE (Acp.)
× Vanda = Vancampe

ADA (Ada)
× Brassia = Brassada
× Cochlioda = Adioda
× Odontoglossum = Adaglossum

ADAGLOSSUM (Adgm.) (Ada × Odontoglossum)

ADIODA (Ado.) (Ada × Cochlioda)

AËRANGIS (Aërgs.)
  × Aëranthes = Thesaëra
  × Angraecum = Angrangis

AËRANTHES (Aërth.)
  × Aërangis = Thesaëra
  × Angraecum = Angranthes

AËRIDACHNIS (Aërdns.) (Aërides × Arachnis)

AËRIDES (Aër.)
  × Arachnis = Aëridachnis
  × Arachnis × Ascocentrum × Vanda = Lewisara
  × Arachnis × Renanthera = Lymanara
  × Arachnis × Rhynchostylis = Sagarikara
  × Arachnis × Trichoglottis = Paulsenara
  × Arachnis × Vanda = Burkillara
  × Ascocentrum = Aëridocentrum
  × Ascocentrum × Renanthera × Vanda = Robinara
  × Ascocentrum × Vanda = Christieara
  × Ascoglossum = Aëridoglossum
  × Doritis = Aëriditis
  × Luisia = Aëridisia
  × Neofinetia = Aëridofinetia
  × Neofinetia × Vanda = Vandofinides
  × Phalaenopsis = Aëridopsis
  × Phalaenopsis × Vanda = Phalaërianda
  × Renanthera = Renades
  × Renanthera × Rhynchostylis = Chewara
  × Renanthera × Vanda = Nobleara
  × Renanthera × Vandopsis = Carterara
  × Rhynchostylis = Rhynchorides
  × Rhynchostylis × Vanda = Perreiraara
  × Vanda = Aëridovanda
  × Vanda × Vandopsis = Maccoyara
  × Vandopsis = Vandopsides

AËRIDISIA (Aërsa.) (Aërides × Luisia)

AËRIDITIS (Aërdts.) (Aërides × Doritis)

AËRIDOCENTRUM (Aërctm.) (Aërides × Ascocentrum)

AËRIDOFINETIA (Aërf.) (Aërides × Neofinetia)

AËRIDOGLOSSUM (Aërgm.) (Aërides × Ascoglossum)

AËRIDOPSIS (Aërps.) (Aërides × Phalaenopsis)

AËRIDOVANDA (Aërdv.) (Aërides × Vanda)

AGANISIA (Agn.)
  × Batemannia × Otostylis × Zygosepalum = Downsara
  × Otostylis = Otonisia

ALICEARA (Alcra.) (Brassia × Miltonia × Oncidium)

ALLENARA (Alna.) (Cattleya × Diacrium × Epidendrum × Laelia)

ANGRAECUM (Angcm.)
  × Aërangis = Angrangis
  × Aëranthes = Angranthes
  × Cyrtorchis = Angraeorchis

ANGRAEORCHIS (Angchs.) (Angraecum × Cyrtorchis)

ANGRANGIS (Angrs.) (Aërangis × Angraecum)

ANGRANTHES (Angth.) (Aëranthes × Angraecum)

ANGULOA (Ang.)
  × Lycaste = Angulocaste

ANGULOCASTE (Angcst.) (Anguloa × Lycaste)

ANOECTOCHILUS (Anct.)
  × Haemaria = Anoectomaria

ANOECTOMARIA (Anctma.) (Anoectochilus × Haemaria)

ANSELLIA (Aslla.)
  × Cymbidium = Ansidium

ANSIDIUM (Asdm.) (Ansellia × Cymbidium)

ARACHNIS (Arach.)
  × Aërides = Aëridachnis
  × Aërides × Ascocentrum × Vanda = Lewisara
  × Aërides × Renanthera = Lymanara
  × Aërides × Rhynchostylis = Sagarikara
  × Aërides × Trichoglottis = Paulsenara
  × Aërides × Vanda = Burkillara
  × Ascocentrum = Ascorachnis
  × Ascocentrum × Renanthera × Vanda = Yusofara
  × Ascocentrum × Rhynchostylis × Vanda = Bovornara
  × Ascocentrum × Vanda = Mokara
  × Ascoglossum = Arachnoglossum
  × Phalaenopsis = Arachnopsis
  × Phalaenopsis × Renanthera = Sappanara

Arachnis (continued)

  × Phalaenopsis × Vanda = Trevorara
  × Phalaenopsis × Vandopsis = Laycockara
  × Renanthera = Aranthera
  × Renanthera × Vanda = Holttumara
  × Renanthera × Vanda × Vandopsis = Teohara
  × Renanthera × Vandopsis = Limara
  × Rhynchostylis = Arachnostylis
  × Trichoglottis = Arachnoglottis
  × Trichoglottis × Vanda = Ridleyara
  × Vanda = Aranda
  × Vanda × Vandopsis = Leeara
  × Vandopsis = Vandachnis

ARACHNOGLOSSUM (Arngm.) (Arachnis × Ascoglossum)

ARACHNOGLOTTIS (Arngl.) (Arachnis × Trichoglottis)

ARACHNOPSIS (Arnps.) (Arachnis × Phalaenopsis)

ARACHNOSTYLIS (Arnst.) (Arachnis × Rhynchostylis)

ARANDA (Aranda) (Arachnis × Vanda)

ARANTHERA (Arnth.) (Arachnis × Renanthera)

ARIZARA (Ariz.) (Cattleya × Domingoa × Epidendrum)

ASCANDOPSIS (Ascdps.) (Ascocentrum × Vandopsis)

ASCOCENDA (Ascda.) (Ascocentrum × Vanda)

ASCOCENTRUM (Asctm.)

  × Aërides = Aëridocentrum
  × Aërides × Arachnis × Vanda = Lewisara
  × Aërides × Renanthera × Vanda = Robinara
  × Aërides × Vanda = Christieara
  × Arachnis = Ascorachnis
  × Arachnis × Renanthera × Vanda = Yusofara
  × Arachnis × Rhynchostylis × Vanda = Bovornara
  × Arachnis × Vanda = Mokara
  × Ascoglossum × Renanthera × Vanda = Shigeuraara
  × Doritis = Doricentrum
  × Doritis × Phalaenopsis = Beardara
  × Doritis × Phalaenopsis × Vanda = Vandewegheara
  × Doritis × Vanda = Ascovandoritis
  × Gastrochilus × Vanda = Eastonara
  × Luisia × Neofinetia = Luascotia

Ascocentrum (continued)
× Luisia × Vanda = Debruyneara
× Neofinetia = Ascofinetia
× Neofinetia × Renanthera = Rosakirschara
× Neofinetia × Rhynchostylis = Rumrillara
× Neofinetia × Vanda = Nakamotoara
× Pelatantheria = Pelacentrum
× Phalaenopsis = Asconopsis
× Phalaenopsis × Renanthera × Vanda = Stamariaara
× Phalaenopsis × Vanda = Devereuxara
× Renanthera = Renancentrum
× Renanthera × Rhynchostylis = Komkrisara
× Renanthera × Vanda = Kagawara
× Renanthera × Vanda × Vandopsis = Onoara
× Rhynchostylis = Rhynchocentrum
× Rhynchostylis × Vanda = Vascostylis
× Sarcochilus = Sarcocentrum
× Trichoglottis × Vanda = Fujioara
× Vanda = Ascocenda
× Vanda × Vandopsis = Wilkinsara
× Vandopsis = Ascandopsis

ASCOFINETIA (Ascf.) (Ascocentrum × Neofinetia)
ASCOGLOSSUM (Ascgm.)
× Aërides = Aëridoglossum
× Arachnis = Arachnoglossum
× Ascocentrum × Renanthera × Vanda = Shigeuraara
× Renanthera = Renanthoglossum
× Vanda = Vanglossum

ASCONOPSIS (Ascps.) (Ascocentrum × Phalaenopsis)

ASCORACHNIS (Ascns.) (Ascocentrum × Arachnis)

ASCOVANDORITIS (Asvts.) (Ascocentrum × Doritis × Vanda)

ASPASIA (Asp.)
× Brassia = Brapasia
× Brassia × Miltonia = Forgetara
× Cochlioda × Odontoglossum = Lagerara
× Miltonia = Milpasia
× Miltonia × Odontoglossum × Oncidium = Withnerara
× Odontoglossum = Aspoglossum
× Oncidium = Aspasium

ASPASIUM (Aspsm.) (Aspasia × Oncidium)

ASPOGLOSSUM (Aspgm.) (Aspasia × Odontoglossum)

BARBOSAARA (Bbra.) (Cochlioda × Gomesa × Odontoglossum × Oncidium)

BARDENDRUM (Bard.) (Barkeria × Epidendrum)

BARKERIA (Bark.)
× Cattleya × Laelia = Laeliocattkeria
× Epidendrum = Bardendrum
× Laelia = Laeliokeria

BATEMANNIA (Btmna.)
× Aganisia × Otostylis × Zygosepalum = Downsara
× Otostylis = Bateostylis
× Otostylis × Zygosepalum = Palmerara
× Zygosepalum = Zygobatemannia*

BATEOSTYLIS (Btst.) (Batemannia × Otostylis)

BEALLARA (Bllra.) (Brassia × Cochlioda × Miltonia × Odontoglossum)

BEARDARA (Bdra.) (Ascocentrum × Doritis × Phalaenopsis)

BIFRENARIA (Bif.)
× Lycaste = Lycasteria

BLETIA (Bletia)

BLETILLA (Ble.)

BLOOMARA (Blma.) (Broughtonia × Laeliopsis × Tetramicra)

BOLLEA (Bol.)
× Chondrorhyncha = Chondrobollea

BOVORNARA (Bov.) (Arachnis × Ascocentrum × Rhynchostylis × Vanda)

BRADEARA (Brade.) (Comparettia × Gomesa × Rodriguezia)

BRAPASIA (Brap.) (Brassia × Aspasia)

BRASSADA (Brsa.) (Ada × Brassia)

BRASSAVOLA (B.)
× Broughtonia = Brassotonia
× Cattleya = Brassocattleya
× Cattleya × Diacrium = Hookerara
× Cattleya × Diacrium × Laelia = Iwanagara
× Cattleya × Epidendrum = Vaughnara
× Cattleya × Epidendrum × Laelia = Yamadara
× Cattleya × Epidendrum × Laelia × Sophronitis = Rothara

Brassavola (continued)
  × Cattleya × Laelia = Brassolaeliocattleya
  × Cattleya × Laelia × Schomburgkia = Recchara
  × Cattleya × Laelia × Sophronitis = Potinara
  × Cattleya × Laeliopsis = Fujiwarara
  × Cattleya × Schomburgkia = Dekensara
  × Cattleya × Sophronitis = Rolfeara
  × Diacrium = Brassodiacrium
  × Epidendrum = Brassoepidendrum
  × Laelia = Brassolaelia
  × Laelia × Sophronitis = Lowara
  × Schomburgkia = Schombavola
  × Sophronitis = Brassophronitis

BRASSIA (Brs.)
  × Ada = Brassada
  × Aspasia = Brapasia
  × Aspasia × Miltonia = Forgetara
  × Cochlioda × Miltonia × Odontoglossum = Beallara
  × Cochlioda × Miltonia × Odontoglossum × Oncidium = Goodaleara
  × Cochlioda × Odontoglossum = Sanderara
  × Miltonia = Miltassia
  × Miltonia × Odontoglossum = Degarmoara
  × Miltonia × Oncidium = Aliceara
  × Odontoglossum = Odontobrassia
  × Oncidium = Brassidium
  × Rodriguezia = Rodrassia

BRASSIDIUM (Brsdm.) (Brassia × Oncidium)

BRASSOCATTLEYA (Bc.) (Brassavola × Cattleya)

BRASSODIACRIUM (Bdia.) (Brassavola × Diacrium)

BRASSOEPIDENDRUM (Bepi.) (Brassavola × Epidendrum)

BRASSOLAELIA (Bl.) (Brassavola × Laelia)

BRASSOLAELIOCATTLEYA (Blc.) (Brassavola × Cattleya × Laelia)

BRASSOPHRONITIS (Bnts.) (Brassavola × Sophronitis)

BRASSOTONIA (Bstna.) (Brassavola × Broughtonia)

BROUGHTONIA (Bro.)
  × Brassavola = Brassotonia
  × Cattleya = Cattleytonia
  × Cattleya × Diacrium = Brownara

Broughtonia (continued)
× Cattleya × Laelia = Laeliocatonia
× Cattleya × Laeliopsis = Osmentara
× Cattleyopsis = Cattleyopsistonia
× Cattleyopsis × Diacrium = Nashara
× Cattleyopsis × Laeliopsis = Gauntlettara
× Diacrium = Diabroughtonia
× Diacrium × Schomburgkia = Shipmanara
× Epidendrum = Epitonia
× Epidendrum × Laeliopsis = Moscosoara
× Laelia = Laelonia
× Laelia × Laeliopsis = Jimenezara
× Laelia × Sophronitis = Hartara
× Laeliopsis = Lioponia
× Laeliopsis × Schomburgkia = Hildaara
× Laeliopsis × Tetramicra = Bloomara
× Schomburgkia = Schombonia
× Tetramicra = Tetratonia

BROWNARA (Bwna.) (Broughtonia × Cattleya × Diacrium)

BULBOPHYLLUM (Bulb.)

BURKILLARA (Burk.) (Aërides × Arachnis × Vanda)

BURRAGEARA (Burr.) (Cochlioda × Miltonia × Odontoglossum × Oncidium)

CALANTHE (Cal.)
× Phaius = Phaiocalanthe

CARTERARA (Ctra.) (Aërides × Renanthera × Vandopsis)

CATAMODES (Ctmds.) (Catasetum × Mormodes)

CATANOCHES (Ctnchs.) (Catasetum × Cycnoches)

CATASETUM (Ctsm.)
× Cycnoches = Catanoches
× Mormodes = Catamodes

CATTLEYA (C.)
× Barkeria × Laelia = Laeliocattkeria
× Brassavola = Brassocattleya
× Brassavola × Diacrium = Hookerara
× Brassavola × Diacrium × Laelia = Iwanagara
× Brassavola × Epidendrum = Vaughnara
× Brassavola × Epidendrum × Laelia = Yamadara
× Brassavola × Epidendrum × Laelia × Sophronitis = Rothara

125

Cattleya (continued)

× Brassavola × Laelia = Brassolaeliocattleya
× Brassavola × Laelia × Schomburgkia = Recchara
× Brassavola × Laelia × Sophronitis = Potinara
× Brassavola × Laeliopsis = Fujiwarara
× Brassavola × Schomburgkia = Dekensara
× Brassavola × Sophronitis = Rolfeara
× Broughtonia = Cattleytonia
× Broughtonia × Diacrium = Brownara
× Broughtonia × Laelia = Laeliocatonia
× Broughtonia × Laeliopsis = Osmentara
× Cattleyopsis × Epidendrum = Hawkesara
× Diacrium = Diacattleya
× Diacrium × Epidendrum × Laelia = Allenara
× Diacrium × Laelia = Dialaeliocattleya
× Diacrium × Schomburgkia = Mizutara
× Domingoa × Epidendrum = Arizara
× Epidendrum = Epicattleya
× Epidendrum × Laelia = Epilaeliocattleya
× Epidendrum × Laelia × Schomburgkia = Northenara
× Epidendrum × Laelia × Sophronitis = Kirchara
× Epidendrum × Schomburgkia = Scullyara
× Epidendrum × Sophronitis = Stacyara
× Laelia = Laeliocattleya
× Laelia × Schomburgkia = Lyonara (1959)
× Laelia × Schomburgkia × Sophronitis = Herbertara
× Laelia × Sophronitis = Sophrolaeliocattleya
× Laeliopsis = Laeliopleya
× Schomburgkia = Schombocattleya
× Sophronitis = Sophrocattleya

CATTLEYOPSIS (Ctps.)
× Broughtonia = Cattleyopsistonia
× Broughtonia × Diacrium = Nashara
× Broughtonia × Laeliopsis = Gauntlettara
× Cattleya × Epidendrum = Hawkesara
× Domingoa = Cattleyopsisgoa

CATTLEYOPSISGOA (Ctpga.) (Cattleyopsis × Domingoa)

CATTLEYOPSISTONIA (Ctpsta.) (Broughtonia × Cattleyopsis)

CATTLEYTONIA (Ctna.) (Broughtonia × Cattleya)

CHARLESWORTHARA (Cha.) (Cochlioda × Miltonia × Oncidium)

CHEWARA (Chew.) (Aërides × Renanthera × Rhynchostylis)

CHONDROBOLLEA (Chdb.) (Chondrorhyncha × Bollea)

CHONDRORHYNCHA (Chdrh.)
× Bollea = Chondrobollea
× Zygopetalum = Zygorhyncha*

CHRISTIEARA (Chtra.) (Aërides × Ascocentrum × Vanda)

CHYSIS (Chy.)

CIRRHOPETALUM (Cirr.)

COCHELLA (Chla.) (Cochleanthes × Mendoncella)

COCHLEANTHES (Cnths.)
× Huntleya = Huntleanthes
× Mendoncella = Cochella
× Pescatorea = Pescoranthes
× Stenia = Cochlenia

COCHLENIA (Cclna.) (Cochleanthes × Stenia)

COCHLIODA (Cda.)
× Ada = Adioda
× Aspasia × Odontoglossum = Lagerara
× Brassia × Miltonia × Odontoglossum = Beallara
× Brassia × Miltonia × Odontoglossum × Oncidium = Goodaleara
× Brassia × Odontoglossum = Sanderara
× Gomesa × Odontoglossum × Oncidium = Barbosaara
× Miltonia = Miltonioda
× Miltonia × Odontoglossum = Vuylstekeara
× Miltonia × Odontoglossum × Oncidium = Burrageara
× Miltonia × Oncidium = Charlesworthara
× Odontoglossum = Odontioda
× Odontoglossum × Oncidium = Wilsonara
× Oncidium = Oncidioda

COELOGYNE (Coel.)

COLAX (Clx.)
× Otostylis = Otocolax
× Zygopetalum = Zygocolax*

COLMANARA (Colm.) (Miltonia × Odontoglossum × Oncidium)

COMPARETTIA (Comp.)
× Gomesa × Rodriguezia = Bradeara
× Ionopsis = Ionettia
× Odontoglossum = Odontorettia
× Oncidium = Oncidettia

ANYONE FOR ORCHIDS?

Blc. Leslie Hoffman 'Ramona' AM/AOS
Grower: Granville Keith

Photo by Beauford B. Fischer

Blc. Greenwich 'Cover Girl'
Rod McLellan Co.

$\times$ Oncidium $\times$ Rodriguezia = Warneara
$\times$ Rodriguezia = Rodrettia

CYCNOCHES (Cyc.)
$\times$ Catasetum = Catanoches
$\times$ Mormodes = Cycnodes

CYCNODES (Cycd.) (Cycnoches $\times$ Mormodes)

CYMBIDIUM (Cym.)
$\times$ Ansellia = Ansidium
$\times$ Grammatophyllum = Grammatocymbidium
$\times$ Phaius = Phaiocymbidium*

CYNORKIS (Cyn.)

CYRTOPODIUM (Cyrt.)

CYRTORCHIS (Cyrtcs.)
$\times$ Angraecum = Angraeorchis

DEBRUYNEARA (Dbra.) (Ascocentrum $\times$ Luisia $\times$ Vanda)

DEGARMOARA (Dgmra.) (Brassia $\times$ Miltonia $\times$ Odontoglossum)

DEKENSARA (Dek.) (Brassavola $\times$ Cattleya $\times$ Schomburgkia)

DENDROBIUM (Den.)

DEVEREUXARA (Dvra.) (Ascocentrum $\times$ Phalaenopsis $\times$ Vanda)

DIABROUGHTONIA (Diab.) (Broughtonia $\times$ Diacrium)

DIACATTLEYA (Diaca.) (Cattleya $\times$ Diacrium)

DIACRIUM (Diacm.)
$\times$ Brassavola = Brassodiacrium
$\times$ Brassavola $\times$ Cattleya = Hookerara
$\times$ Brassavola $\times$ Cattleya $\times$ Laelia = Iwanagara
$\times$ Broughtonia = Diabroughtonia
$\times$ Broughtonia $\times$ Cattleya = Brownara
$\times$ Broughtonia $\times$ Cattleyopsis = Nashara
$\times$ Broughtonia $\times$ Schomburgkia = Shipmanara
$\times$ Cattleya = Diacattleya
$\times$ Cattleya $\times$ Epidendrum $\times$ Laelia = Allenara
$\times$ Cattleya $\times$ Laelia = Dialaeliocattleya
$\times$ Cattleya $\times$ Schomburgkia = Mizutara
$\times$ Epidendrum = Epidiacrium
$\times$ Laelia = Dialaelia
$\times$ Laeliopsis = Dialaeliopsis
$\times$ Schomburgkia = Schombodiacrium

DIALAELIA (Dial.) (Diacrium × Laelia)

DIALAELIOCATTLEYA (Dialc.) (Cattleya × Diacrium × Laelia)

DIALAELIOPSIS (Dialps.) (Diacrium × Laeliopsis)

DILLONARA (Dill.) (Epidendrum × Laelia × Schomburgkia)

DISA (Disa)

DOMINDESMIA (Ddma.) (Domingoa × Hexadesmia)

DOMINGOA (Dga.)
  × Cattleya × Epidendrum = Arizara
  × Cattleyopsis = Cattleyopsisgoa
  × Epidendrum = Epigoa
  × Hexadesmia = Domindesmia
  × Laeliopsis = Domliopsis

DOMLIOPSIS (Dmlps.) (Domingoa × Laeliopsis)

DORICENTRUM (Dctm.) (Ascocentrum × Doritis)

DORIELLA (Drlla.) (Doritis × Kingiella)

DORIELLAOPSIS (Dllps.) (Doritis × Kingiella × Phalaenopsis)

DORIFINETIA (Dfta.) (Doritis × Neofinetia)

DORITAENOPSIS (Dtps.) (Doritis × Phalaenopsis)

DORITIS (Dor.)
  × Aërides = Aëriditis
  × Ascocentrum = Doricentrum
  × Ascocentrum × Phalaenopsis = Beardara
  × Ascocentrum × Phalaenopsis × Vanda = Vandewegheara
  × Ascocentrum × Vanda = Ascovandoritis
  × Kingiella = Doriella
  × Kingiella × Phalaenopsis = Doriellaopsis
  × Neofinetia = Dorifinetia
  × Phalaenopsis = Doritaenopsis
  × Phalaenopsis × Rhynchostylis = Rhyndoropsis
  × Phalaenopsis × Vanda = Hagerara
  × Phalaenopsis × Vandopsis = Hausermannara
  × Renanthera = Dorthera
  × Vanda = Vandoritis

DORTHERA (Dtha.) (Doritis × Renanthera)

DOSSINIA (Doss.)
  × Haemaria = Dossinimaria

DOSSINIMARIA (Dsma.) (Dossinia × Haemaria)

130

DOWNSARA (Dwsa.) (Aganisia × Batemannia × Otostylis × Zygosepalum)

EASTONARA (Eas.) (Ascocentrum × Gastrochilus × Vanda)

EPICATTLEYA (Epc.) (Cattleya × Epidendrum)

EPIDELLA (Epdla.) (Epidendrum × Nageliella)

EPIDENDRUM (Epi.)
× Barkeria = Bardendrum
× Brassavola = Brassoepidendrum
× Brassavola × Cattleya = Vaughnara
× Brassavola × Cattleya × Laelia = Yamadara
× Brassavola × Cattleya × Laelia × Sophronitis = Rothara
× Broughtonia = Epitonia
× Broughtonia × Laeliopsis = Moscosoara
× Cattleya = Epicattleya
× Cattleya × Cattleyopsis = Hawkesara
× Cattleya × Domingoa = Arizara
× Cattleya × Epidendrum × Laelia = Allenara
× Cattleya × Laelia = Epilaeliocattleya
× Cattleya × Laelia × Schomburgkia = Northenara
× Cattleya × Laelia × Sophronitis = Kirchara
× Cattleya × Schomburgkia = Scullyara
× Cattleya × Sophronitis = Stacyara
× Diacrium = Epidiacrium
× Domingoa = Epigoa
× Laelia = Epilaelia
× Laelia × Schomburgkia = Dillonara
× Laelia × Sophronitis = Stanfieldara
× Laeliopsis = Epilaeliopsis
× Nageliella = Epidella
× Schomburgkia = Schomboepidendrum
× Sophronitis = Epiphronitis

EPIDIACRIUM (Epdcm.) (Diacrium × Epidendrum)

EPIGOA (Epg.) (Domingoa × Epidendrum)

EPILAELIA (Epl.) (Epidendrum × Laelia)

EPILAELIOCATTLEYA (Eplc.) (Cattleya × Epidendrum × Laelia)

EPILAELIOPSIS (Eplps.) (Epidendrum × Laeliopsis)

EPIPHRONITIS (Ephs.) (Epidendrum × Sophronitis)

EPITONIA (Eptn.) (Broughtonia × Epidendrum)

ERNESTARA (Entra.) (Phalaenopsis × Renanthera × Vandopsis)

131

EULOPHIELLA (Eul.)

FORGETARA (Fgtra.) (Aspasia × Brassia × Miltonia)

FUJIOARA (Fjo.) (Ascocentrum × Trichoglottis × Vanda)

FUJIWARARA (Fjw.) (Brassavola × Cattleya × Laeliopsis)

GASTROCHILUS (Gchls.)
  × Ascocentrum × Vanda = Eastonara
  × Sarcochilus = Gastrosarcochilus

GASTROSARCOCHILUS (Gsarco.) (Gastrochilus × Sarcochilus)

GAUNTLETTARA (Gtra.) (Broughtonia × Cattleyopsis × Laeliopsis)

GOFFARA (Gfa.) (Luisia × Rhynchostylis × Vanda)

GOMESA (Gom.)
  × Cochlioda × Odontoglossum × Oncidium = Barbosaara
  × Comparettia × Rodriguezia = Bradeara
  × Macradenia = Macradesa
  × Oncidium = Oncidesa

GOODALEARA (Gdlra.) (Brassia × Cochlioda × Miltonia × Odontoglossum × Oncidium)

GRAMMATOCYMBIDIUM (Grcym.) (Cymbidium × Grammato-phyllum)

GRAMMATOPHYLLUM (Gram.)
  × Cymbidium = Grammatocymbidium

HABENARIA (Hab.)

HAEMARIA (Haem.)
  × Anoectochilus = Anoectomaria
  × Dossinia = Dossinimaria
  × Macodes = Macomaria

HAGERARA (Hgra.) (Doritis × Phalaenopsis × Vanda)

HARTARA (Hart.) (Broughtonia × Laelia × Sophronitis)

HAUSERMANNARA (Haus.) (Doritis × Phalaenopsis × Vandopsis)

HAWAIIARA (Haw.) (Renanthera × Vanda × Vandopsis)

HAWKESARA (Hwkra.) (Cattleya × Cattleyopsis × Epidendrum)

HERBERTARA (Hbtr.) (Cattleya × Laelia × Schomburgkia × Sophronitis)

HEXADESMIA (Hex.)
× Domingoa = Domindesmia

HILDAARA (Hdra.) (Broughtonia × Laeliopsis × Schomburgkia)

HOLTTUMARA (Holtt.) (Arachnis × Renanthera × Vanda)

HOOKERARA (Hook.) (Brassavola × Cattleya × Diacrium)

HOWEARA (Hwra.) (Leochilus × Oncidium × Rodriguezia)

HUEYLIHARA (Hylra.) (Neofinetia × Renanthera × Rhyncho-stylis)

HUNTLEANTHES (Hnths.) (Cochleanthes × Huntleya)

HUNTLEYA (Hya.)
× Cochleanthes = Huntleanthes

IONETTIA (Intta.) (Comparettia × Ionopsis)

IONOCIDIUM (Incdm.) (Ionopsis × Oncidium)

IONOPSIS (Inps.)
× Comparettia = Ionettia
× Oncidium = Ionocidium
× Rodriguezia = Rodriopsis

IWANAGARA (Iwan.) (Brassavola × Cattleya × Diacrium × Laelia)

JIMENEZARA (Jmzra.) (Broughtonia × Laelia × Laeliopsis)

JOANNARA (Jnna.) (Renanthera × Rhynchostylis × Vanda)

KAGAWARA (Kgw.) (Ascocentrum × Renanthera × Vanda)

KINGIELLA (King.)
× Doritis = Doriella
× Doritis × Phalaenopsis = Doriellaopsis
× Phalaenopsis = Phaliella

KIRCHARA (Kir.) (Cattleya × Epidendrum × Laelia × Sophronitis)

KOMKRISARA (Kom.) (Ascocentrum × Renanthera × Rhyncho-stylis)

LAELIA (L.)
× Barkeria = Laeliokeria
× Barkeria × Cattleya = Laeliocattkeria

133

Laelia (continued)
× Brassavola = Brassolaelia
× Brassavola × Cattleya = Brassolaeliocattleya
× Brassavola × Cattleya × Diacrium = Iwanagara
× Brassavola × Cattleya × Epidendrum = Yamadara
× Brassavola × Cattleya × Epidendrum × Sophronitis = Rothara
× Brassavola × Cattleya × Schomburgkia = Recchara
× Brassavola × Cattleya × Sophronitis = Potinara
× Brassavola × Sophronitis = Lowara
× Broughtonia = Laelonia
× Broughtonia × Cattleya = Laeliocatonia
× Broughtonia × Laeliopsis = Jimenezara
× Broughtonia × Sophronitis = Hartara
× Cattleya = Laeliocattleya
× Cattleya × Diacrium = Dialaeliocattleya
× Cattleya × Diacrium × Epidendrum = Allenara
× Cattleya × Epidendrum = Epilaeliocattleya
× Cattleya × Epidendrum × Schomburgkia = Northenara
× Cattleya × Epidendrum × Sophronitis = Kirchara
× Cattleya × Schomburgkia = Lyonara (1959)
× Cattleya × Schomburgkia × Sophronitis = Herbertara
× Cattleya × Sophronitis = Sophrolaeliocattleya
× Diacrium = Dialaelia
× Epidendrum = Epilaelia
× Epidendrum × Schomburgkia = Dillonara
× Epidendrum × Sophronitis = Stanfieldara
× Laeliopsis = Liaopsis
× Leptotes = Leptolaelia
× Schomburgkia = Schombolaelia
× Sophronitis = Sophrolaelia

LAELIOCATONIA (Lctna.) (Broughtonia × Cattleya × Laelia)

LAELIOCATTKERIA (Lcka.) (Barkeria × Cattleya × Laelia)

LAELIOCATTLEYA (Lc.) (Cattleya × Laelia)

LAELIOKERIA (Lkra.) (Barkeria × Laelia)

LAELIOPLEYA (Lpya.) (Cattleya × Laeliopsis)

LAELIOPSIS (Lps.)
× Brassavola × Cattleya = Fujiwarara
× Broughtonia = Lioponia
× Broughtonia × Cattleya = Osmentara
× Broughtonia × Cattleyopsis = Gauntlettara
× Broughtonia × Laelia = Jimenezara

Laeliopsis (continued)
   × Broughtonia × Epidendrum = Moscosoara
   × Broughtonia × Schomburgkia = Hildaara
   × Broughtonia × Tetramicra = Bloomara
   × Cattleya = Laeliopleya
   × Diacrium = Dialaeliopsis
   × Domingoa = Domliopsis
   × Epidendrum = Epilaeliopsis
   × Laelia = Liaopsis
   × Tetramicra = Tetraliopsis

LAELONIA (Lna.) (Broughtonia × Laelia)

LAGERARA (Lgra.) (Aspasia × Cochlioda × Odontoglossum)

LAYCOCKARA (Lay.) (Arachnis × Phalaenopsis × Vandopsis)

LEEARA (Leeara) (Arachnis × Vanda × Vandopsis)

LEOCHILUS (Lchs.)
   × Oncidium = Leocidium
   × Oncidium × Rodriguezia = Howeara

LEOCIDIUM (Lcdm.) (Leochilus × Oncidium)

LEPANTHES (Lths.)

LEPTOLAELIA (Lptl.) (Laelia × Leptotes)

LEPTOTES (Lpt.)
   × Laelia = Leptolaelia

LEWISARA (Lwsra.) (Aërides × Arachnis × Ascocentrum × Vanda)

LIAOPSIS (Liaps.) (Laelia × Laeliopsis)

LIMARA (Lim.) (Arachnis × Renanthera × Vandopsis)

LIOPONIA (Lpna.) (Broughtonia × Laeliopsis)

LOWARA (Low.) (Brassavola × Laelia × Sophronitis)

LUASCOTIA (Lscta.) (Ascocentrum × Luisia × Neofinetia)

LUINETIA (Lnta.) (Luisia × Neofinetia)

LUINOPSIS (Lnps.) (Luisia × Phalaenopsis)

LUISANDA (Lsnd.) (Luisia × Vanda)

LUISIA (Lsa.)
   × Aërides = Aëridisia
   × Ascocentrum × Neofinetia = Luascotia

Luisia (continued)
  × Ascocentrum × Vanda = Debruyneara
  × Neofinetia = Luinetia
  × Phalaenopsis = Luinopsis
  × Pomatocalpa = Pomatisia
  × Rhynchostylis × Vanda = Goffara
  × Vanda = Luisanda

LUTHERARA (Luth.) (Phalaenopsis × Renanthera × Rhynchostylis)

LYCASTE (Lyc.)
  × Anguloa = Angulocaste
  × Bifrenaria = Lycasteria
  × Maxillaria = Maxillacaste
  × Zygopetalum = Zygocaste*

LYCASTERIA (Lystr.) (Bifrenaria × Lycaste)

LYMANARA (Lymra.) (Aërides × Arachnis × Renanthera)

LYONARA (1959 not 1948) **(Lyon.) (Cattleya × Laelia × Schomburgkia)**

MACCOYARA (Mcyra.) (Aërides × Vanda × Vandopsis)

MACODES (Mac.)
  × Haemaria = Macomaria
MACRADENIA (Mcdn.)
  × Gomesa = Macradesa
  × Oncidium = Oncidenia
  × Rodriguezia = Rodridenia

MACRADESA (Mcdsa.) (Gomesa × Macradenia)

MASDEVALLIA (Masd.)

MAXILLACASTE (Mxcst.) (Lycaste × Maxillaria)

MAXILLARIA (Max.)
  × Lycaste = Maxillacaste

MENDONCELLA (Mdcla.)
  × Cochleanthes = Cochella
  × Zygopetalum = Zygocella*

MILPASIA (Mpsa.) (Aspasia × Miltonia)

MILPILIA (Mpla.) (Miltonia × Trichopilia)

MILTASSIA (Mtssa.) (Brassia × Miltonia)

MILTONIA (Milt.)
 × Aspasia = Milpasia
 × Aspasia × Brassia = Forgetara
 × Aspasia × Odontoglossum × Oncidium = Withnerara
 × Brassia = Miltassia
 × Brassia × Cochlioda × Odontoglossum = Beallara
 × Brassia × Cochlioda × Odontoglossum × Oncidium = Goodaleara
 × Brassia × Odontoglossum = Degarmoara
 × Brassia × Oncidium = Aliceara
 × Cochlioda = Miltonioda
 × Cochlioda × Odontoglossum = Vuylstekeara
 × Cochlioda × Odontoglossum × Oncidium = Burrageara
 × Cochlioda × Oncidium = Charlesworthara
 × Odontoglossum = Odontonia
 × Odontoglossum × Oncidium = Colmanara
 × Oncidium = Miltonidium
 × Rodriguezia = Rodritonia
 × Trichopilia = Milpilia

MILTONIDIUM (Mtdm.) (Miltonia × Oncidium)

MILTONIODA (Mtda.) (Cochlioda × Miltonia)

MIZUTARA (Miz.) (Cattleya × Diacrium × Schomburgkia)

MOIRARA (Moir.) (Phalaenopsis × Renanthera × Vanda)

MOKARA (Mkra.) (Arachnis × Ascocentrum × Vanda)

MORMODES (Morm.)
 × Cycnoches = Cycnodes
 × Catasetum = Catamodes

MOSCOSOARA (Mscra.) (Broughtonia × Epidendrum × Laeliopsis)

NAGELIELLA (Ngl.)
 × Epidendrum = Epidella

NAKAMOTOARA (Nak.) (Ascocentrum × Neofinetia × Vanda)

NASHARA (Nash.) (Broughtonia × Cattleyopsis × Diacrium)

NEOFINETIA (Neof.)
 × Aërides = Aëridofinetia
 × Aërides × Vanda = Vandofinides
 × Ascocentrum = Ascofinetia
 × Ascocentrum × Luisia = Luascotia
 × Ascocentrum × Renanthera = Rosakirschara
 × Ascocentrum × Rhynchostylis = Rumrillara
 × Ascocentrum × Vanda = Nakamotoara

Neofinetia (continued)
   × Doritis = Dorifinetia
   × Luisia = Luinetia
   × Phalaenopsis = Phalanetia
   × Renanthera = Renanetia
   × Renanthera × Rhynchostylis = Hueylihara
   × Rhynchostylis = Neostylis
   × Vanda = Vandofinetia

NEOSTYLIS (Neost.) (Neofinetia × Rhynchostylis)

NOBLEARA (Nlra.) (Aërides × Renanthera × Vanda)

NORTHENARA (Nrna.) (Cattleya × Epidendrum × Laelia × Schomburgkia)

ODONTIODA (Oda.) (Cochlioda × Odontoglossum)

ODONTOBRASSIA (Odbrs.) (Brassia × Odontoglossum)

ODONTOCIDIUM (Odcdm.) (Odontoglossum × Oncidium)

ODONTOGLOSSUM (Odm.)
   × Ada = Adaglossum
   × Aspasia = Aspoglossum
   × Aspasia × Cochlioda = Lagerara
   × Aspasia × Miltonia × Oncidium = Withnerara
   × Brassia = Odontobrassia
   × Brassia × Cochlioda = Sanderara
   × Brassia × Cochlioda × Miltonia = Beallara
   × Brassia × Cochlioda × Miltonia × Oncidium = Goodaleara
   × Brassia × Miltonia = Degarmoara
   × Cochlioda = Odontioda
   × Cochlioda × Gomesa × Oncidium = Barbosaara
   × Cochlioda × Miltonia = Vuylstekeara
   × Cochlioda × Miltonia × Oncidium = Burrageara
   × Cochlioda × Oncidium = Wilsonara
   × Comparettia = Odontorettia
   × Miltonia = Odontonia
   × Miltonia × Oncidium = Colmanara
   × Oncidium = Odontocidium
   × Rodriguezia = Rodriglossum

ODONTONIA (Odtna.) (Miltonia × Odontoglossum)

ODONTORETTIA (Odrta.) (Comparettia × Odontoglossum)

ONCIDENIA (Oncna.) (Macradenia × Oncidium)

ONCIDESA (Oncsa.) (Gomesa × Oncidium)

ONCIDETTIA (Onctta.) (Comparettia × Oncidium)

ONCIDIODA (Oncda.) (Cochlioda × Oncidium)

ONCIDIUM (Onc.)
  × Aspasia = Aspasium
  × Aspasia × Miltonia × Odontoglossum = Withnerara
  × Brassia = Brassidium
  × Brassia × Cochlioda × Miltonia × Odontoglossum = Goodaleara
  × Brassia × Miltonia = Aliceara
  × Cochlioda = Oncidioda
  × Cochlioda × Gomesa × Odontoglossum = Barbosaara
  × Cochlioda × Miltonia = Charlesworthara
  × Cochlioda × Miltonia × Odontoglossum = Burrageara
  × Cochlioda × Odontoglossum = Wilsonara
  × Comparettia = Oncidettia
  × Comparettia × Rodriguezia = Warneara
  × Gomesa = Oncidesa
  × Ionopsis = Ionocidium
  × Leochilus = Leocidium
  × Leochilus × Rodriguezia = Howeara
  × Macradenia = Oncidenia
  × Miltonia = Miltonidium
  × Miltonia × Odontoglossum = Colmanara
  × Odontoglossum = Odontocidium
  × Ornithophora = Ornithocidium
  × Rodriguezia = Rodricidium
  × Trichocentrum = Trichocidium
  × Trichopilia = Oncidpilia

ONCIDPILIA (Oncpa.) (Oncidium × Trichopilia)

**ONOARA (Onra.) (Ascocentrum × Renanthera × Vanda ×
  Vandopsis)**

OPSISANDA (Opsis.) (Vanda × Vandopsis)

OPSISTYLIS (Opst.) (Rhynchostylis × Vandopsis)

ORCHIS (Orchis)

ORNITHOCIDIUM (Orncm.) (Oncidium × Ornithophora)

ORNITHOPHORA (Orpha.)
  × Oncidium = Ornithocidium

OSMENTARA (Osmt.) (Broughtonia × Cattleya × Laeliopsis)

OTOCOLAX (Otcx.) (Colax × Otostylis)

OTONISIA (Otnsa.) (Aganisia × Otostylis)

OTOSEPALUM (Otspm.) (Otostylis × Zygosepalum)

OTOSTYLIS (Otst.)
× Aganisia = Otonisia
× Aganisia × Batemannia × Zygosepalum = Downsara
× Batemannia = Bateostylis
× Batemannia × Zygosepalum = Palmerara
× Colax = Otocolax
× Zygopetalum = Zygostylis*
× Zygosepalum = Otosepalum

PALMERARA (Plmra.) (Batemannia × Otostylis × Zygosepalum)

PAPHIOPEDILUM (Paph.)
× Phragmipedium = Phragmipaphium

PARACHILUS (Prcls.) (Parasarcochilus × Sarcochilus)

PARASARCOCHILUS (Psarco.)
× Sarcochilus = Parachilus

PAULSENARA (Plsra.) (Aërides × Arachnis × Trichoglottis)

PELACENTRUM (Plctm.) (Ascocentrum × Pelatantheria)

PELATANTHERIA (Pthia.)
× Ascocentrum = Pelacentrum

PERREIRAARA (Prra.) (Aërides × Rhynchostylis × Vanda)

PESCATOREA (Pes.)
× Cochleanthes = Pescoranthes

PESCORANTHES (Psnth.) (Cochleanthes × Pescatorea)

PHAIOCALANTHE (Phcal.) (Calanthe × Phaius)

PHAIOCYMBIDIUM* (Phycm.) (Cymbidium × Phaius)

PHAIUS (Phaius)
× Calanthe = Phaiocalanthe
× Cymbidium = Phaiocymbidium*

PHALAENOPSIS (Phal.)
× Aërides = Aëridopsis
× Aërides × Vanda = Phalaërianda
× Arachnis = Arachnopsis
× Arachnis × Renanthera = Sappanara
× Arachnis × Vanda = Trevorara

Phalaenopsis (continued)
× Arachnis × Vandopsis = Laycockara
× Ascocentrum = Asconopsis
× Ascocentrum × Doritis = Beardara
× Ascocentrum × Doritis × Vanda = Vandewegheara
× Ascocentrum × Renanthera × Vanda = Stamariaara
× Ascocentrum × Vanda = Devereuxara
× Doritis = Doritaenopsis
× Doritis × Kingiella = Doriellaopsis
× Doritis × Rhynchostylis = Rhyndoropsis
× Doritis × Vanda = Hagerara
× Doritis × Vandopsis = Hausermannara
× Kingiella = Phaliella
× Luisia = Luinopsis
× Neofinetia = Phalanetia
× Renanthera = Renanthopsis
× Renanthera × Rhynchostylis = Lutherara
× Renanthera × Vanda = Moirara
× Renanthera × Vandopsis = Ernestara
× Rhynchostylis = Rhynchonopsis
× Rhynchostylis × Vanda = Yapara
× Sarcochilus = Sarconopsis
× Vanda = Vandaenopsis
× Vandopsis = Phalandopsis

PHALAËRIANDA (Phda.) (Aërides × Phalaenopsis × Vanda)

PHALANDOPSIS (Phdps.) (Phalaenopsis × Vandopsis)

PHALANETIA (Phnta.) (Neofinetia × Phalaenopsis)

PHALIELLA (Phlla.) (Kingiella × Phalaenopsis)

PHRAGMIPAPHIUM (Phrphm.) (Paphiopedilum × Phragmipedium)

PHRAGMIPEDIUM (Phrag.)
× Paphiopedilum = Phragmipaphium

PLEIONE (Pln.)

POLYSTACHYA (Pol.)

POMATISIA (Pmtsa.) (Luisia × Pomatocalpa)

POMATOCALPA (Pmcpa.)
× Luisia = Pomatisia

POTINARA (Pot.) (Brassavola × Cattleya × Laelia × Sophronitis)

141

PROMENAEA (Prom.)
 × Zygopetalum = Propetalum

PROPETALUM (Pptm.) (Promenaea × Zygopetalum)

RECCHARA (Recc.) (Brassavola × Cattleya × Laelia × Schomburgkia)

RENADES (Rnds.) (Aërides × Renanthera)

RENAGLOTTIS (Rngl.) (Renanthera × Trichoglottis)

RENANCENTRUM (Rnctm.) (Ascocentrum × Renanthera)

RENANETIA (Rnet.) (Neofinetia × Renanthera)

RENANOPSIS (Rnps.) (Renanthera × Vandopsis)

RENANSTYLIS (Rnst.) (Renanthera × Rhynchostylis)

RENANTANDA (Rntda.) (Renanthera × Vanda)

RENANTHERA (Ren.)
 × Aërides = Renades
 × Aërides × Arachnis = Lymanara
 × Aërides × Ascocentrum × Vanda = Robinara
 × Aërides × Rhynchostylis = Chewara
 × Aërides × Vanda = Nobleara
 × Aërides × Vandopsis = Carterara
 × Arachnis = Aranthera
 × Arachnis × Ascocentrum × Vanda = Yusofara
 × Arachnis × Phalaenopsis = Sappanara
 × Arachnis × Vanda = Holttumara
 × Arachnis × Vanda × Vandopsis = Teohara
 × Arachnis × Vandopsis = Limara
 × Ascocentrum = Renancentrum
 × Ascocentrum × Ascoglossum × Vanda = Shigeuraara
 × Ascocentrum × Neofinetia = Rosakirschara
 × Ascocentrum × Phalaenopsis × Vanda = Stamariaara
 × Ascocentrum × Rhynchostylis = Komkrisara
 × Ascocentrum × Vanda = Kagawara
 × Ascocentrum × Vanda × Vandopsis = Onoara
 × Ascoglossum = Renanthoglossum
 × Doritis = Dorthera
 × Neofinetia = Renanetia
 × Neofinetia × Rhynchostylis = Hueylihara
 × Phalaenopsis = Renanthopsis
 × Phalaenopsis × Rhynchostylis = Lutherara

Renanthera (continued)
  × Phalaenopsis × Vanda = Moirara
  × Phalaenopsis × Vandopsis = Ernestara
  × Rhynchostylis = Renanstylis
  × Rhynchostylis × Vanda = Joannara
  × Rhynchostylis × Vandopsis = Yoneoara
  × Sarcochilus = Sarcothera
  × Trichoglottis = Renaglottis
  × Vanda = Renantanda
  × Vanda × Vandopsis = Hawaiiara
  × Vandopsis = Renanopsis

RENANTHOGLOSSUM (Rngm.) (Ascoglossum × Renanthera)

RENANTHOPSIS (Rnthps.) (Phalaenopsis × Renanthera)

RHINERRHIZA (Rhin.)
  × Sarcochilus = Rhinochilus

RHINOCHILUS (Rhincs.) (Rhinerrhiza × Sarcochilus)

RHYNCHOCENTRUM (Rhctm.) (Ascocentrum × Rhynchostylis)

RHYNCHONOPSIS (Rhnps.) (Phalaenopsis × Rhynchostylis)

RHYNCHORIDES (Rhrds.) (Aërides × Rhynchostylis)

RHYNCHOSTYLIS (Rhy.)
  × Aërides = Rhynchorides
  × Aërides × Arachnis = Sagarikara
  × Aërides × Renanthera = Chewara
  × Aërides × Vanda = Perreiraara
  × Arachnis = Arachnostylis
  × Arachnis × Ascocentrum × Vanda = Bovornara
  × Ascocentrum = Rhynchocentrum
  × Ascocentrum × Neofinetia = Rumrillara
  × Ascocentrum × Renanthera = Komkrisara
  × Ascocentrum × Vanda = Vascostylis
  × Doritis × Phalaenopsis = Rhyndoropsis
  × Luisia × Vanda = Goffara
  × Neofinetia = Neostylis
  × Neofinetia × Renanthera = Hueylihara
  × Phalaenopsis = Rhynchonopsis
  × Phalaenopsis × Renanthera = Lutherara
  × Phalaenopsis × Vanda = Yapara
  × Renanthera = Renanstylis
  × Renanthera × Vanda = Joannara
  × Renanthera × Vandopsis = Yoneoara

Rhynchostylis (continued)
  × Sarcochilus = Sartylis
  × Vanda = Rhynchovanda
  × Vandopsis = Opsistylis

RHYNCHOVANDA (Rhv.) (Rhynchostylis × Vanda)

RHYNDOROPSIS (Rhdps.) (Doritis × Phalaenopsis × Rhynchostylis)

RIDLEYARA (Ridl.) (Arachnis × Trichoglottis × Vanda)

ROBINARA (Rbnra.) (Aërides × Ascocentrum × Renanthera × Vanda)

RODRASSIA (Rdssa.) (Brassia × Rodriguezia)

RODRETTIA (Rdtta.) (Comparettia × Rodriguezia)

RODRICIDIUM (Rdcm.) (Oncidium × Rodriguezia)

RODRIDENIA (Rden.) (Macradenia × Rodriguezia)

RODRIGLOSSUM (Rdgm.) (Odontoglossum × Rodriguezia)

RODRIGUEZIA (Rdza.)
  × Brassia = Rodrassia
  × Comparettia = Rodrettia
  × Comparettia × Gomesa = Bradeara
  × Comparettia × Oncidium = Warneara
  × Ionopsis = Rodriopsis
  × Leochilus × Oncidium = Howeara
  × Macradenia = Rodridenia
  × Miltonia = Rodritonia
  × Odontoglossum = Rodriglossum
  × Oncidium = Rodricidium

RODRIOPSIS (Rodps.) (Ionopsis × Rodriguezia)

RODRITONIA (Rdtna.) (Miltonia × Rodriguezia)

ROLFEARA (Rolf.) (Brassavola × Cattleya × Sophronitis)

ROSAKIRSCHARA (Rskra.) (Ascocentrum × Neofinetia × Renanthera)

ROTHARA (Roth.) (Brassavola × Cattleya × Epidendrum × Laelia × Sophronitis)

RUMRILLARA (Rlla.) (Ascocentrum × Neofinetia × Rhynchostylis)

SAGARIKARA (Sgka.) (Aërides × Arachnis × Rhynchostylis)

SANDERARA (Sand.) (Brassia × Cochlioda × Odontoglossum)

SAPPANARA (Sapp.) (Arachnis × Phalaenopsis × Renanthera)

SARCOCENTRUM (Srctm.) (Ascocentrum × Sarcochilus)

SARCOCHILUS (Sarco.)
    × Ascocentrum = Sarcocentrum
    × Gastrochilus = Gastrosarcochilus
    × Parasarcochilus = Parachilus
    × Phalaenopsis = Sarconopsis
    × Renanthera = Sarcothera
    × Rhinerrhiza = Rhinochilus
    × Rhynchostylis = Sartylis
    × Vanda = Sarcovanda

SARCONOPSIS (Srnps.) (Phalaenopsis × Sarcochilus)

SARCOTHERA (Srth.) (Renanthera × Sarcochilus)

SARCOVANDA (Srv.) (Sarcochilus × Vanda)

SARTYLIS (Srts.) (Rhynchostylis × Sarcochilus)

SCHOMBAVOLA (Smbv.) (Brassavola × Schomburgkia)

SCHOMBOCATTLEYA (Smbc.) (Cattleya × Schomburgkia)

SCHOMBODIACRIUM (Smbdcm.) (Diacrium × Schomburgkia)

SCHOMBOEPIDENDRUM (Smbep.) (Epidendrum × Schomburgkia)

SCHOMBOLAELIA (Smbl.) (Laelia × Schomburgkia)

SCHOMBONIA (Smbna.) (Broughtonia × Schomburgkia)

SCHOMBONITIS (Smbts.) (Schomburgkia × Sophronitis)

SCHOMBURGKIA (Schom.)
    × Brassavola = Schombavola
    × Brassavola × Cattleya = Dekensara
    × Brassavola × Cattleya × Laelia = Recchara
    × Broughtonia = Schombonia
    × Broughtonia × Diacrium = Shipmanara
    × Broughtonia × Laeliopsis = Hildaara
    × Cattleya = Schombocattleya
    × Cattleya × Diacrium = Mizutara
    × Cattleya × Epidendrum = Scullyara
    × Cattleya × Epidendrum × Laelia = Northenara
    × Cattleya × Laelia = Lyonara (1959)
    × Cattleya × Laelia × Sophronitis = Herbertara

Schomburgkia (continued)
  × Diacrium = Schombodiacrium
  × Epidendrum = Schomboepidendrum
  × Epidentrum × Laelia = Dillonara
  × Laelia = Schombolaelia
  × Sophronitis = Schombonitis

SCULLYARA (Scu.) (Cattleya × Epidendrum × Schomburgkia)

SHIGEURAARA (Shgra.) (Ascocentrum × Ascoglossum × Renanthera × Vanda)

SHIPMANARA (Shipm.) (Broughtonia × Diacrium × Schomburgkia)

SOBRALIA (Sob.)

SOPHROCATTLEYA (Sc.) (Cattleya × Sophronitis)

SOPHROLAELIA (Sl.) (Laelia × Sophronitis)

SOPHROLAELIOCATTLEYA (Slc.) (Cattleya × Laelia × Sophronitis)

SOPHRONITIS (Soph.)
  × Brassavola = Brassophronitis
  × Brassavola × Cattleya = Rolfeara
  × Brassavola × Cattleya × Epidendrium × Laelia = Rothara
  × Brassavola × Cattleya × Laelia = Potinara
  × Brassavola × Laelia = Lowara
  × Broughtonia × Laelia = Hartara
  × Cattleya = Sophrocattleya
  × Cattleya × Epidendrum = Stacyara
  × Cattleya × Epidendrum × Laelia = Kirchara
  × Cattleya × Laelia = Sophrolaeliocattleya
  × Cattleya × Laelia × Schomburgkia × Herbertara
  × Epidendrum = Epiphronitis
  × Epidendrum × Laelia = Stanfieldara
  × Laelia = Sophrolaelia
  × Schomburgkia = Schombonitis

SPATHOGLOTTIS (Spa.)

STACYARA (Stac.) (Cattleya × Epidendrum × Sophronitis)

STAMARIAARA (Stmra.) (Ascocentrum × Phalaenopsis × Renanthera × Vanda)

STANFIELDARA (Sfdra.) (Epidendrum × Laelia × Sophronitis)

STANHOPEA (Stan.)

STENIA (Stenia)
 × Cochleanthes = Cochlenia

TEOHARA (Thra.) (**Arachnis** × **Renanthera** × **Vanda** × **Vandopsis**)

TETRALIOPSIS (Ttps.) (**Laeliopsis** × **Tetramicra**)

TETRAMICRA (Ttma.)
 × Broughtonia = Tetratonia
 × Broughtonia × Laeliopsis = Bloomara
 × Laeliopsis = Tetraliopsis

TETRATONIA (Ttna.) (**Broughtonia** × **Tetramicra**)

THESAËRA (Thsra.) (**Aërangis** × **Aëranthes**)

THUNIA (Thu.)

TREVORARA (Trev.) (**Arachnis** × **Phalaenopsis** × **Vanda**)

TRICHOCENTRUM (Trctm.)
 × Oncidium = Trichocidium

TRICHOCIDIUM (Trcdm.) (**Oncidium** × **Trichocentrum**)

TRICHOGLOTTIS (Trgl.)
 × Aërides × Arachnis = Paulsenara
 × Arachnis = Arachnoglottis
 × Arachnis × Vanda = Ridleyara
 × Ascocentrum × Vanda = Fujioara
 × Renanthera = Renaglottis
 × Vanda = Trichovanda
 × Vandopsis = Trichopsis

TRICHOPILIA (Trpla.)
 × Miltonia = Milpilia
 × Oncidium = Oncidpilia

TRICHOPSIS (Trcps.) (**Trichoglottis** × **Vandopsis**)

TRICHOVANDA (Trcv.) (**Trichoglottis** × **Vanda**)

VANCAMPE (Vcp.) (**Acampe** × **Vanda**)

VANDA (V.)
 × Acampe = Vancampe
 × Aërides = Aëridovanda
 × Aërides × Arachnis = Burkillara
 × Aërides × Arachnis × Ascocentrum = Lewisara
 × Aërides × Ascocentrum = Christieara
 × Aërides × Ascocentrum × Renanthera = Robinara
 × Aërides × Neofinetia = Vandofinides

Vanda (continued)
× Aërides × Phalaenopsis = Phalaërianda
× Aërides × Renanthera = Nobleara
× Aërides × Rhynchostylis = Perreiraara
× Aërides × Vandopsis = Maccoyara
× Arachnis = Aranda
× Arachnis × Ascocentrum = Mokara
× Arachnis × Ascocentrum × Renanthera = Yusofara
× Arachnis × Ascocentrum × Rhynchostylis = Bovornara
× Arachnis × Phalaenopsis = Trevorara
× Arachnis × Renanthera = Holttumara
× Arachnis × Renanthera × Vandopsis = Teohara
× Arachnis × Trichoglottis = Ridleyara
× Arachnis × Vandopsis = Leeara
× Ascocentrum = Ascocenda
× Ascocentrum × Ascoglossum × Renanthera = Shigeuraara
× Ascocentrum × Doritis = Ascovandoritis
× Ascocentrum × Doritis × Phalaenopsis = Vandewegheara
× Ascocentrum × Gastrochilus = Eastonara
× Ascocentrum × Luisia = Debruyneara
× Ascocentrum × Neofinetia = Nakamotoara
× Ascocentrum × Phalaenopsis = Devereuxara
× Ascocentrum × Phalaenopsis × Renanthera = Stamariaara
× Ascocentrum × Renanthera = Kagawara
× Ascocentrum × Renanthera × Vandopsis = Onoara
× Ascocentrum × Rhynchostylis = Vascostylis
× Ascocentrum × Trichoglottis = Fujioara
× Ascocentrum × Vandopsis = Wilkinsara
× Ascoglossum = Vanglossum
× Doritis = Vandoritis
× Doritis × Phalaenopsis = Hagerara
× Luisia = Luisanda
× Luisia × Rhynchostylis = Goffara
× Neofinetia = Vandofinetia
× Phalaenopsis = Vandaenopsis
× Phalaenopsis × Renanthera = Moirara
× Phalaenopsis × Rhynchostylis = Yapara
× Renanthera = Renantanda
× Renanthera × Rhynchostylis = Joannara
× Renanthera × Vandopsis = Hawaiiara
× Rhynchostylis = Rhynchovanda
× Sarcochilus = Sarcovanda
× Trichoglottis = Trichovanda
× Vandopsis = Opsisanda

VANDACHNIS (Vchns.) (Arachnis × Vandopsis)

VANDAENOPSIS (Vdnps.) (Phalaenopsis × Vanda)

VANDEWEGHEARA (Vwga.) (Ascocentrum × Doritis × Phalaenopsis × Vanda)

VANDOFINETIA (Vf.) (Neofinetia × Vanda)

VANDOFINIDES (Vfds.) (Aërides × Neofinetia × Vanda)

VANDOPSIDES (Vdpsd.) (Aërides × Vandopsis)

VANDOPSIS (Vdps.)
- × Aërides = Vandopsides
- × Aërides × Renanthera = Carterara
- × Aërides × Vanda = Maccoyara
- × Arachnis = Vandachnis
- × Arachnis × Phalaenopsis = Laycockara
- × Arachnis × Renanthera = Limara
- × Arachnis × Renanthera × Vanda = Teohara
- × Arachnis × Vanda = Leeara
- × Ascocentrum = Ascandopsis
- × Ascocentrum × Renanthera × Vanda = Onoara
- × Ascocentrum × Vanda = Wilkinsara
- × Doritis × Phalaenopsis = Hausermannara
- × Phalaenopsis = Phalandopsis
- × Phalaenopsis × Renanthera = Ernestara
- × Renanthera = Renanopsis
- × Renanthera × Rhynchostylis = Yoneoara
- × Renanthera × Vanda = Hawaiiara
- × Rhynchostylis = Opsistylis
- × Trichoglottis = Trichopsis
- × Vanda = Opsisanda

VANDORITIS (Vdts.) (Doritis × Vanda)

VANGLOSSUM (Vgm.) (Ascoglossum × Vanda)

VASCOSTYLIS (Vasco.) (Ascocentrum × Rhynchostylis × Vanda)

VAUGHNARA (Vnra.) (Brassavola × Cattleya × Epidendrum)

VUYLSTEKEARA (Vuyl.) (Cochlioda × Miltonia × Odonto-glossum)

WARNEARA (Wnra.) (Comparettia × Oncidium × Rodriguezia)

WILKINSARA (Wknsra.) (Ascocentrum × Vanda × Vandopsis)

WILSONARA (Wils.) (Cochlioda × Odontoglossum × Oncidium)

WITHNERARA (With.) (Aspasia × Miltonia × Odontoglossum × Oncidium)

YAMADARA (Yam.) (Brassavola × Cattleya × Epidendrum × Laelia)

YAPARA (Yap.) (Phalaenopsis × Rhynchostylis × Vanda)

YONEOARA (Ynra.) (Renanthera × Rhynchostylis × Vandopsis)

YUSOFARA (Ysfra.) (Arachnis × Ascocentrum × Renanthera × Vanda)

ZYGOBATEMANNIA* (Zbm.) (Batemannia × Zygopetalum)

ZYGOCASTE* (Zcst.) (Lycaste × Zygopetalum)

ZYGOCELLA* (Zcla.) (Mendoncella × Zygopetalum)

ZYGOCOLAX* (Zcx.) (Colax × Zygopetalum)

ZYGOPETALUM* (Z.)
   × Batemannia = Zygobatemannia*
   × Chondrorhyncha = Zygorhyncha*
   × Colax = Zygocolax*
   × Lycaste = Zygocaste*
   × Mendoncella = Zygocella*
   × Otostylis = Zygostylis*
   × Promenaea = Propetalum

ZYGORHYNCHA* (Zcha.) (Chondrorhyncha × Zygopetalum)

ZYGOSEPALUM (Zspm.)
   × Aganisia × Batemannia × Otostylis = Downsara
   × Batemannia × Otostylis = Palmerara
   × Otostylis = Otosepalum

ZYGOSTYLIS* (Zsts.) (Otostylis × Zygopetalum)

* An opinion is that one or more or all of the grexes registered in the genera indicated thus * are of suspect acceptability

I X
Awards and Judging

AWARDS

Awards are given or have been given to orchids by the following Societies:

  AOS—American Orchid Society
  ODC—Orchid Digest Corporation
  RHS—Royal Horticultural Society
  SFOS—South Florida Orchid Society
  HOS—Honolulu Orchid Society
  FWCOS—Florida West Coast Orchid Society
  CSA—Cymbidium Society of America
  2 WOC—Second World Orchid Conference
  5 WOC—Fifth World Orchid Conference
  7 WOC—Seventh World Orchid Conference
  8 WOC—Eighth World Orchid Conference
  2 HOC—Second Hawaiian Orchid Conference
  OSSC—Orchid Society of Southern California
  OST—Orchid Society of Thailand
  MOS—Malayan Orchid Society
  RHT—Royal Horticultural Society of Thailand
  RSPC—Siam Society of Plant Culture
  TOS—Taiwan Orchid Society
  SMOS—South Malaysia Orchid Society
  DOG—Deutschen Orchideen-Gesellschaft

The following excerpt from the AOS Handbook on Judging and Exhibition, 5th edition, gives the reader a clear view of the process and purpose of judging orchid plants and flowers.

If you live near a Regional or Supplemental Judging Center, you will be welcomed as a visitor or exhibitor. You will learn much from these sessions. Addresses of AOS regional judging are included in this chapter.

151

PURPOSES AND CATEGORIES OF A. O. S. AWARDS

Since the judging of orchids is such an exacting art, it is important to follow the exact procedures set forth by the American Orchid Society. Therefore, these rules are presented from the American Orchid Society handbook on judging.

The awards of the American Orchid Society, Inc., are designed both to recognize and to encourage meritorious achievements in all fields of orchid endeavor. To accomplish this, Awards are granted to individual persons, to individual orchid plants, to groups of orchid plants, to cut orchid flowers, and to orchid arrangements, all in accordance with established procedures. Wherever such Awards are determined by point scores, the appropriate American Orchid Society Point Scale shall be used consistent with American Orchid Society Judging Practice. Awards which are granted to individual plants are made to that one particular clone which must be designated by a cultivar name. All divisions of that clone, whether made prior or subsequent to the granting of the award, bear that award and the same cultivar name, although only the originally judged portion receives a Certificate.

All American Orchid Society Awards are granted only by the American Orchid Society, Inc., either by vote of the Trustees or upon the scoring and/or decision of the American Orchid Society Judges.

American Orchid Society Awards may be made only by American Orchid Society Judges in accordance with the rules of the American Orchid Society, Inc., under certain circumstances:

(1) At show tables of the American Orchid Society, Inc., or shows given by the Society.
(2) At regional or international orchid congresses and conferences.
(3) At regional and subregional monthly judging.
(4) At recognized annual shows of Affiliated Societies.
(5) At established major public flower shows or orchid shows.

Awards are either in the form of medals or engraved Certificates, as indicated below:

Medals

Gold Medal of Achievement: Awarded by vote of the Trustees of the American Orchid Society, Inc., upon recommendation, to individuals for distinguished work in orchid culture or in scientific research on orchids; and for outstanding services to the Society.

Silver Medal of Merit: Awarded by vote of the Trustees of the American Orchid Society, Inc., upon recommendation, to individuals in recognition of outstanding service to the American Orchid Society or some major contribution to the orchid world.

Certificates

Gold, Silver and Bronze Medal Certificates: Awarded to groups, collections or cut-flower exhibits according to the following scoring:

Gold Medal Certificate	Score of 91 points or over
Silver Medal Certificate	Score of 86 points to 90 points
Bronze Medal Certificate	Score of 80–85 points

(Note: Point Scale used is #12, Groups of Plants or Cut Flowers Arranged for Effect, page 00.)

Bronze Medal Certificate (for Meritorious Educational Exhibit): Awarded to an educational exhibit of outstanding excellence which scores 90 points or over (Point Scale used is #13, Educational Exhibit).

Bronze Medal Certificate (for Meritorious Flower Arrangement): Awarded to an outstanding exhibit in the Flower Arrangement Class in which orchid flowers are dominant. Only upon recommendation of the Flower Arrangement Judges and upon unanimous decision of the American Orchid Society Judges shall the award be granted, with the following stipulations:

(1) there shall be no limitation in size;
(2) orchids must be dominant;
(3) orchid flowers need not have been raised by the exhibitor.

Bronze Medal Certificate (for Meritorious Display of Orchids in Use): Awarded to an outstanding exhibit of not less than 25 square feet which the judges consider to be exceptionally artistic. No restriction shall apply as to the class of the exhibitor, whether amateur, commercial, or professional florist. The award shall be given only upon unanimous decision

ANYONE FOR ORCHIDS?

Odontioda Aloette 'Granados'
HCC/AOS

Vanda sanderana 'Tomio' AM/AOS

Dendrobium Helen Fukumura
'Adrienne' AM/AOS

Phalaenopsis Xylophone 'Peppermint Candy' HCC/AOS
Rod McLellan Co.

Cymbidium Burgundian 'Chateau'
FCC/AOS

of the judging team assigned. Judges are expected to consider the exhibit with Point Scale #14 ("Orchid Arrangements") in mind, and, although actual scoring is optional, no award should be made to an exhibit which the judge feels could not receive at least 80 points according to Point Scale #14.

First Class Certificate: Awarded to orchid species or hybrids of outstanding excellence which score 90 points or over (Point Scales used are #1 to #9 inclusive).

Award of Merit: Awarded to orchid species or hybrids of outstanding excellence which score at least 80 but less than 90 points (Point Scales used are #1 to #9 inclusive).

Highly Commended Certificate: Awarded to orchid species or hybrids of unusual distinctiveness which score just below 80 points, but not less than 75 points (Point Scales used are #1 to #9 inclusive).

Judges' Commendation: Awarded to orchid plants or flowers, individually or in groups, which in the opinion of the judges have some notable quality they are unable to score. Judges' written commendation must record the specific value or values for which the award is given. Granted unanimously by the team of judges without scoring.

Award of Distinction: Given once to a cross, exhibited individually or severally, representing a worthy new direction in breeding. Granted by a unanimous decision, without scoring, of the judging team assigned. Both the hybridizer and exhibitor, if different, will receive a Certificate.

Award of Quality: Given once to a cross, exhibited as a group of not less than 12 plants or the inflorescences thereof, of a raised species or hybrid which may or may not have been made before when the result is sufficient improvement over the former type. Granted by a unanimous decision, without scoring, of the judging team assigned. Both the hybridizer and exhibitor, if different, will receive a Certificate.

Certificate of Cultural Merit: Awarded to a specimen plant of robust health and an unusually large number of flowers. Must score 80 points or over (Point Scale used is #10, Cultural Merit).

Certificate of Botanical Merit: Awarded only to well-grown plants of uncommon species which, by virtue of possessing one or more outstanding characteristics or one or more characteristics in outstanding degree, represent a worthy new concept of horticultural desirability. Must score 80 points or over (Point Scale used is #11, Botanical Merit). This Certificate may be granted more than once to the same species if different clones have significantly different characteristics. It is required that the written record of every C.B.M. award include, whenever possible, reference to an authoritative source of identification.

Trophy

Show Trophy for the Most Outstanding Orchid Exhibit: A Show Award intended to encourage the improvement of the standards of exhibits is made available to Annual Shows of domestic Affiliated Societies and to other major shows within the United States upon request.   The following regulations apply:

(1) Only Certified American Orchid Society Judges may participate in awarding the Trophy.

(2) To be eligible for consideration an exhibit must cover a minimum of 25 square feet.

(3) To be eligible to receive this award an exhibit must be of such quality that, if scored according to Point Scale #12 (see page 166), it would receive at least 80 points. It shall be the responsibility of the Chairman of A. O. S. judges to remind all judges present of these regulations and to provide them with official ballots for their use in awarding the Trophy. Ballots will be made available in sufficient number to every Show which requests the Trophy as part of the Judging Kit. Point Scale #12 will be printed on each ballot for reference.

(4) If a Judge feels that no exhibit in the Show merits the Award, it is expected that this opinion will be noted in writing on the ballot. If a Judge casts a ballot in favor of making the Award to an exhibit, it shall be assumed that the Judge is satisfied that the exhibit meets at least the minimum criteria with respect to area (25 square feet) and quality (80 points).

(5) If ballots in favor of awarding the Show Trophy are received from at least two-thirds (2/3) of the Judges who are present and voting, the Trophy will be awarded to

the exhibit which receives a majority of the votes cast. In case of a tie, or in instances where no majority is obtained, ballots may be recast.

(6) If more than one-third (1/3) of the Judges vote against giving the Trophy to any exhibit, the Trophy must be withheld, as it is not the intent that awarding it shall be obligatory.

Show Trophy Certificate

Show Trophy Certificate for the Most Outstanding Orchid Exhibit: A Show Award intended to encourage the improvement of the standards of exhibits is made available to Annual Shows of Affiliated Societies outside the United States of America, upon request. The following stipulations apply: either A. O. S. Judges who may be present or judges who are recognized in their country to be well-qualified, but who need not be A. O. S. Judges, may award this certificate to an exhibit which covers a minimum of 25 square feet (2.25 square meters).

CRITERIA FOR JUDGING THE
MAJOR ORCHID GENERA

The Point Scales on the following pages cover the major horticultural types of orchids, as well as the manner of exhibiting, so as to afford a standardized basis for the consideration of judges in granting any kind of American Orchid Society award which needs to be scored. In all instances where qualities of orchids are to be scored, the following concepts must be borne in mind by the judges as criteria for the various genera or generic types.

Cattleya and Allied Genera: The general form of the flower of fine varieties is toward fullness and roundness, that is, a circumscribed circle drawn with the base of the column as the center would touch the tips of the petals and sepals and the margin of the lip, while the flower would fill the greater proportion of the area of the circle. The sepals should arrange themselves almost in an equilateral triangle while the petals and lip should do likewise but inverted, the sepals being broad and filling in the gap between the petals and the petals and the lip. The petals should be erect (but not too stiff) to slightly arching (but not drooping), broad and rounded, frilled or undulated at the margins according to variety but not crumpled and folded. The lip should be proportionate to the petals according to variety (brassocattleyas, for example, generally have lips larger than the petals; most cattleyas, laelias, and laeliocattleyas have lips slightly smaller than the petals, depending on the ancestral species used), with a rounded, flattened, symmetrical and crisped or frilled trumpet but closed toward the base and more or less rolled around the column. The entire flower should be fairly flat when viewed from the side, the lip curving down and not jutting out at right angles to the plane of the petals and sepals.

The color of the flower generally should be clear, bright and strong, evenly dispersed throughout the petals and sepals without "washing out" at the mid-veins, of a hue in keeping with the parentage or an unusual shade if handsome and desirable, without spotting, breaking or splashing except where a balanced and harmonious pattern adds distinction. The lip should be more prominently and more richly colored, with symmetrical pattern if additionally marked, the whole lip blending or pleasingly contrasting with the rest of the flower.

The size of the flower should be equal to or greater than the average size of the parents. The potential of the species in size, in total or in parts may already have been established by fine forms discovered in their natural habitats.

Substance of a high degree, through polyploid forms, is now the standard.

Texture should be sparkling, crystalline, velvety or waxy.

Floriferousness is closely related to parental background and size of flowers. While cattleyas with one exceptional flower may be judged, labiata-type cattleyas preferably should have two or more flowers to be considered. In crosses involving biofoliate cattleyas, several flowers would have to be produced to warrant consideration, depending on the ancestry involved.

Stem, in cattleyas, refers to a strong, upright stem which displays the flowers to their best advantage, so that one flower does not crowd and distort another.

In bifoliate crosses, the size of the flowers and the width of the petals will be less than in pure labiata crosses because of the differences of the species involved.

Cymbidium: The general form of the flower is toward round-ness and fullness, as in *Cattleya* but not to the same degree, with some fine cultivars tending toward a more open star-like appearance and other good forms being somewhat cupped, excessive cupping, however, being a fault. The lip usually is not extended to the line of the circumscribed circle, and the dorsal sepal oft-times is not, due to being curved forward or hooded. The sepals should be broad and arranged nearly in an equilateral triangle, filling in the gaps between the petals and lip. The petals usually make an inverted, broadly based isosceles triangle with the lip and should be broad, slightly arched with a minimum of narrowing toward the tips. The lip should be proportionately sized, the side lobes more or less erect, the front lobe curved gracefully but not abruptly turned under nor narrowed or pinched.

The color of the flower should be definite and clear; suffusion of one color over another should be regular and harmonious, not mottled or muddy. Veining with color, if present, should be definite and distinctive, or in regular lines and patterns. The lip should be as distinctively colored as the sepals and petals, with markings in definite and distinctive patterns, the throat and crests clear white or brightly colored.

The size of the flower should be equal to or greater than the average size of the parents.

Substance must be greater than the average of the parents. It is beyond that of the species.

The inflorescence should be erect or gracefully arching, according to ancestral species, with the flowers well spaced and well displayed. The number of the flowers will vary according to the variety and breeding.

Dendrobium: The genus *Dendrobium* is extremely large and diverse, so that general criteria for all species and hybrids cannot be stated. However, the flowers presented for judging generally fall into one of three categories:

In judging species and hybrids of the form typified by *Dendrobium nobile,* the criteria used in judging *Cattleya* flowers would apply.

In judging species and hybrids of the form typified by *Dendrobium phalaenopsis,* the criteria used in judging flowers of the genus *Phalaenopsis* would apply.

In judging those dendrobiums which have petals and sepals

more or less equal, the chief criterion is improvement over the ancestral species.

Miltonia: The general form of the flower is toward fullness, roundness and flatness. The sepals and petals should be equal and only slightly reflexed. The lip should be predominently large, symmetrical and not too deeply notched. Color should be definite, clear and free of blemish. The mask, if present, should be symmetrical and well defined.

The inflorescence should be gracefully arching, with the flowers well spaced and well displayed.

The point scale for *Miltonia* is designed for use in scoring *Miltonia, Oncidium, Odontoglossum* and similar genera whose flowers have lips which are the dominant feature. For other types of miltonias, etc., whose flowers have lips which are proportionate to the other flower segments, the *Odontoglossum* point scale should be used.

Odontoglossum: The general form of the flower is toward roundness, fullness and flatness, tending to fit within a circumscribed circle as in *Cattleya*. The color of the flower must be definite and clear, in well-defined patterns.

Size of flowers should be equal to or greater than the average of the parents.

Substance must be greater than the average of the parents.

The habit of the inflorescence may be simple or branching, with flowers well spaced and well displayed. If branching, there should be no crowding of the flowers.

Floriferousness is closely related to parental background.

The *Odontoglossum* point scale is designed primarily for the *crispum*-type odontoglossums, odontiodas, vuylstekearas, oncidiums, miltonias and similar orchids the flowers of which have lips approximately equal to the other floral segments. For large-lipped forms, score by the *Miltonia* point scale.

Paphiopedilum: The general form of the flowers is toward roundness and fullness, with particular emphasis upon balance and proportion of the segments. The dorsal sepal should be large, rounded, slightly concave and not reflexed.

The ventral sepal may be inconspicuous or can afford a harmonious background for the lip, or as nearly as possible duplicate the dorsal sepal. The petals should be broad and not too long, in proportion with the rest of the flower. The pouch should be in proportion to the rest of the flower.

The color of the flower should be definite, in well-defined areas and patterns.

Due to polyploidy, substance in paphiopedilums generally is heavy and is now accepted with little consideration of this feature.

Texture should be waxy or varnished in the petals and pouch.

Stem should be proportionately long and strong, in relation to the size of the flower.

Size is based on width of the dorsal sepal and the proportions of the rest of the flower to this measurement, according to breeding.

Phalaenopsis: The general form of the flower is toward roundness, fullness, and flatness. The sepals should arrange themselves almost in an equilateral triangle, the dorsal sepal tending to be somewhat larger and broader than the lateral sepals. The petals should be broad and flat, filling in the gap between the sepals, the mid-veins preferably horizontal. The lip will vary according to variety and breeding.

The color, when present on petals and sepals, should be definite and clear and markings, when present, should be pleasing. The lip should be distinctively marked or colored.

The size of the flower should be equal to or greater than the average of the parents.

Substance must be greater than the average of the parents. It is beyond that of the species.

The inflorescence should be gracefully arching, according to breeding, with the flowers well spaced and well displayed. The number of flowers will vary according to the species or, in the case of hybrids, the breeding. A sufficient number of flowers should be open so that their arrangement and presentation can be properly judged and so that they show the full potential of the flower.

Vanda: The general form of the flower is toward roundness, fullness and flatness. The sepals should be broad and rounded, and should arrange themselves almost in an equilateral triangle; the dorsal sepal should be as nearly equal to the lateral sepals as possible. The petals should be broad and rounded, as nearly equal to the dorsal sepal as possible, and should fill the gaps between the sepals. The lips, in size and shape, should be harmonious with the rest of the flower, in accordance with the ancestral species.

The color of the flower should be definite and clear, suffusion of one color over another should be regular and harmonious, not mottled or muddy. Veining with color, if present, should be definite and distinctive, or in regular lines and patterns. The lip should be distinctively colored. The size of the flower should be equal to or greater than the average of the parents.

Substance must be greater than the average of the parents.

The inflorescence should be erect or gracefully arching, according to parental background, with the flower well spaced and displayed. The number of the flowers will vary according to the species or, in the case of hybrids, the breeding.

Spray-types should have a sufficient number of flowers open for the judges to determine the arrangement of the flowers in the inflorescence and mature enough to show the full potential of the flower.

POINT SCALES FOR A. O. S. AWARDS

1. GENERAL POINT SCALE

Form of Flower	30
Color of Flower	30
Other Characteristics	
Size of Flower	10
Substance and Texture	10
Habit and Arrangement of Inflorescence	10
Floriferousness	10
Total Points	**100**

This Point Scale may be used for any genus of orchid except *Paphiopedilum,* and note slight difference in *Cattleya* scale. The special point scales for the genera that follow are recommended but judges' use of the above is optional.

2. CATTLEYAS

Form of Flower		30
General Form	15	
Sepals	5	
Petals	5	
Labellum	5	

Color of Flower			30
General Color	15		
Sepals and Petals	7		
Labellum	8		
Other Characteristics			40
Size of Flower		10	
Substance and Texture		20	
Floriferousness and Stem		10	
		Total Points	100

3. CYMBIDIUMS

Form of Flower			30
General Form	15		
Sepals	5		
Petals	5		
Labellum	5		
Color of Flower			30
General Color	15		
Sepals and Petals	8		
Labellum	7		
Other Characteristics			40
Size of Flower		10	
Substance and Texture		10	
Habit and Arrangement of Inflorescence		10	
Floriferousness		10	
		Total Points	100

4. PAPHIOPEDILUMS

Form of Flower		40
General Form	20	
Sepals	10	
Petals	5	
Pouch	5	
Color of Flower		40
General Color	20	
Sepals	10	
Petals	5	
Pouch	5	

Other Characteristics				20
Size of Flower		10		
Substance and Texture		5		
Stem		5		
			Total Points	100

5. DENDROBIUMS

Form of Flower				30
General Form	15			
Sepals	5			
Petals	5			
Labellum	5			
Color of Flower				30
General Color	15			
Sepals	5			
Petals	5			
Labellum	5			
Other Characteristics				40
Size of Flower		10		
Substance and Texture		10		
Habit and Arrangement of				
Inflorescence		10		
Floriferousness		10		
			Total Points	100

6. MILTONIAS

Form of Flower				30
General Form	15			
Sepals and Petals	6			
Labellum	9			
Color of Flower				30
General Color	15			
Sepals and Petals	6			
Labellum	9			
Other Characteristics				40
Size of Flower		10		
Substance and Texture		10		
Habit and Arrangement of				
Inflorescence		10		
Floriferousness		10		
			Total Points	100

7. ODONTOGLOSSUMS

Form of Flower		30
General Form	15	
Sepals	5	
Petals	5	
Labellum	5	
Color of Flower		30
General Color	15	
Sepals	5	
Petals	5	
Labellum	5	
Other Characteristics		40
Size of Flower	10	
Substance and Texture	10	
Habit and Arrangement of Inflorescence	10	
Floriferousness	10	
Total Points		100

8. PHALAENOPSIS

Form of Flower		30
General Form	15	
Sepals	5	
Petals	6	
Labellum	4	
Color of Flower		30
General Color	15	
Sepals and Petals	10	
Labellum	5	
Other Characteristics		40
Size of Flower	10	
Substance and Texture	10	
Habit and Arrangement of Inflorescence	10	
Floriferousness	10	
Total Points		100

9. VANDAS

Form of Flower			30
General Form	15		
Sepals	7		
Petals	5		
Labellum	3		
Color of Flower			30
General Color	15		
Sepals	7		
Petals	5		
Labellum	3		
Other Characteristics			40
Size of Flower		10	
Substance and Texture		10	
Habit and Arrangement of Inflorescence		10	
Floriferousness		10	
		Total Points	100

10. CULTURAL MERIT

Size and Condition of Plant		50
Floriferousness		30
Quality of Bloom		20
	Total Points	100

11. BOTANICAL MERIT

Flower Characteristics		
Form		12
Color		12
Size		12
Plant Characteristics		
Robustness (size, natural vigor)		10
Condition (culture)		10
Floriferousness		10
Other Characteristics		
Esthetic appeal (charm)		12
Educational value		12
Rarity in cultivation		10
	Total Points	100

12. GROUPS OF PLANTS OR CUT FLOWERS ARRANGED FOR EFFECT

General Arrangement	35
Quality of Flowers	35
Variety	20
Labelling	10
Total Points	100

13. EDUCATIONAL EXHIBIT

Originality of Concept	35
Effectiveness of Presentation	25
Clarity of Labelling and Explanation	25
Appropriateness and Attractiveness of Staging	15
Total Points	100

14. ORCHID ARRANGEMENTS

Scale designed to recognize aesthetic skill in use of orchid flowers, rather than horticultural achievement.

Design   30
>   To include:
>   Balance and Proportion
>   Rhythm
>   Dominance and Contrast

Harmony   30
>   of Color
>   Texture
>   Relation to Container

Conformance to Schedule and/or Suitability of Purpose	15
Distinction	10
Originality	10
Condition	5
Total Points	100

METHODS OF MEASUREMENT AND DESCRIPTION

In the past, the methods of measuring flower size or of recording other descriptive data have varied somewhat in different geographical areas. To facilitate the keeping of comparable records on awards and to develop a clearer understanding of these records, a uniform set of standards is essential. The following outline represents a summary of the most useful concepts and techniques generally agreed upon.

Descriptions of the awards should include the following data with all measurements of plants and flowers to be made in units of the metric system.

1. **Overall Measurement.** (Natural spread of flower). Measurement is made from the extreme outer margin of each petal without changing the natural carriage of the flower.
2. **Actual Measurements**
   a. **Dorsal sepal: width.** The actual maximum dimension across when the sepal is flattened into a plane.
      Length. The actual maximum dimension from point of attachment to tip along the central vein.
   b. **Petal: width and length.** Same as in dorsal sepal.
   c. **Lateral sepal: width and length.** Same as in dorsal sepal. Not needed with paphiopedilums.
   d. **Lip: width.** The actual maximum dimension across the lip in its normal position.
      Length. Measurement extends from the point of attachment at the column-foot to the tip (or to a line representing the outermost margin of the lip).
3. **Color of flower.** The hue, its clarity and intensity, and any pattern or markings on sepals, petals and lip.
4. **Substance and texture of flower.** See definitions of "substance" and "texture."
5. **Number of flowers.** Record number of flowers and number of buds on stem, number of inflorescences if more than one, and total number of flowers for cultural awards.
6. **Arrangement of flowers on stem.** Indicate whether well spaced, clustered, etc.

ANYONE FOR ORCHIDS?

AMERICAN ORCHID SOCIETY REGIONAL JUDGING

Northeast Regional Judging—A. O. S. Judging, c/o L. W. Zimmerman, the Pennsylvania Horticultural Society, 325 Walnut St., Philadelphia, Pa. 19106.

Northeast Supplemental Judging, New York—Snuff Mill, The New York Botanical Garden, Bronx Park, New York, N.Y. at 7:30 p.m. 10458. *(Cut flowers should be sent to the New York Botanical Garden c/o Mr. Robert Russo.)*

Northeast Supplemental Judging, Washington, D.C.—U.S. National Arboretum, 24th and R Streets, N.E., Washington, D.C. *(Plants or cut flowers should be sent to Dr. John Creech, Director, U.S. National Arboretum, Washington, D.C.)*

Mid-America Regional Judging—Community Room, Farm and Home Savings Association, 7801 Forsythe Avenue, Clayton (St. Louis), Missouri 63105. *(Plants or cut flowers should be sent to Mrs. Walter Stern, 11710 Lindemere Drive, St. Louis, Missouri 63131.)*

Mid-America Supplemental Judging, Michigan—Botanical Gardens of the University of Michigan, 1800 Dixboro Road, Ann Arbor, Michigan 48104. *(Plants or cut flowers should be sent to Mr. Raymond McCullough, 14800 Harrison, Livonia, Michigan 48154.)*

Mid-America Supplemental Judging, Georgia—Fernbank Science Center, 156 Heaton Park Drive, N.E., Atlanta, Georgia 30307. *(Cut flowers should be sent to Orchid Judging, c/o Fernbank Science Center at the same address.)*

Pacific Northwest Regional Judging—Greenwood Library, 8016 Greenwood, Seattle, Washington, at 7:00 p.m. *(Plants or cut flowers should be sent to Mrs. Clare J. Seaman, 1502 N.W. 57th Street, Seattle, Washington 98107.)*

Pacific Central Regional Judging*—Lakeside Garden Center, Lakeside Park, Oakland, Calif. *(Send packages to Mrs. Bertie De Martini, c/o Rod McLellan Co., 1450 El Camino Real, So. San Francisco, Calif. 94080.)*

Pacific Central Supplemental Judging*—Hall of Flowers, Golden Gate Park at Lincoln Way and 9th St., San Francisco, Calif. *(Plants or cut flowers should be sent to Mrs. Michael Roccaforte, 414 Naples St., San Francisco, Calif. 94112.)*

Pacific South Regional Judging*—Natural History Museum, Exposition Park, 900 Exposition Boulevard, Los Angeles, California 90007. *(Plants or cut flowers should be sent to Mr. Robert B. Spangenberg, Natural History Museum.)*

Pacific South Supplemental Judging*—Wardlow Park, 3457 Stanbridge, Long Beach, Calif. *(Plants and flowers should be sent to Paul Brecht, 1989 Harbor Blvd., Costa Mesa, Calif. 92627.)*

Southeast Regional Judging—Polish American Club of Miami, 1250 N.W. 22nd Avenue, Miami, Florida. *(Plants or flowers may be sent directly to Jones & Scully Inc., 2200 N.W. 33rd Ave., Miami, Fla. 33142.)*

Southeast Supplemental Judging—The Tampa Garden Center, Conservatory Room, 2629 Bayshore Boulevard, Tampa, Florida. *(Plants or flowers should be sent to Mr. C. C. Curry, P.O. Box 22581, Tampa, Florida 33622.)*

Southwest Regional Judging—Garden Center, 3310 N. New Braunfels Ave., San Antonio, Texas. *(Plants and flowers should be sent to Alamo Orchids, 214 Austin Highway, San Antonio, Texas 78215.)*

Hawaii Regional Judging—Lyon Orchid Garden, Foster Botanical Gardens, Honolulu, Hawaii 96814. *(Cut flowers should be sent to Mr. J. Milton Warne, 260 Jack Lane, Honolulu, Hawaii 96817.)*

Hawaii Supplemental Judging, Hilo—Orchidarium Hawaii, 524 Manana St., Hilo, Hawaii 96720.

Hawaii Supplemental Judging, Maui—Lahaina Civic Center, Lahaina, Maui, Hawaii. *(Cut flowers should be sent to 9 W. Papa Ave., Kahului, Maui, Hawaii 96732.)*

Polyrrhiza lindenii

Photo by Ted Dully

Leafless orchid—a real curiosity

X
Upgrading

Sooner or later you will want to expand your collection to include whatever takes your fancy. I hesitate to give lists of connoisseur plants for fear that some people will decide to start with them. Those of us who have been "at this" for some time know the pitfalls of starting out at the end rather than at the beginning.

If you attend orchid society meetings or do a lot of visiting you will see plants you like. Try one or two and see how you do with them. If you can grow an easy Cattleya, try an expensive awarded one. Buy and bloom one Slc before you rush out and buy ten and find out you don't have enough light.

Don't start out on a rare and scarce plant and have its death on your conscience. Besides, most of us would rather grow a well known plant to perfection than have a lot of poorly grown rarities hanging on for dear life. Before buying a rare species do enough research and talk to people who grow it to make sure you understand its needs and can provide it with the right environmental niche.

Grow the genera until you understand its growing habits and cycles. This will give you the experience to try to expand into a rare or hard to grow one.

For example, Masdevallia are a current rage. We've all killed our share of them. A case in point is my own early experience with Masdevallias. I thought they were darling and though I was a novice window sill grower, I bought several. Needless to say, they all croaked. Later, I got one really going—75 or so blooms on a plant in a 3 inch pot. One day it was thriving and blooming its head off. The next day there was a circle of dead leaves surrounding a bare plant. It was probably a bacterial infection that strikes with amazing rapidity. Sure they have enchanting crazy flowers, but go slow, buy one, try another, etc. Don't just rush out and buy all the Masdevallias in a catalogue.

Paphiopedilum Betty Bracy 'Treva' HCC/AOS

Blc. Malworth 'Orchidglade' FCC/AOS
Jones and Scully, Inc.

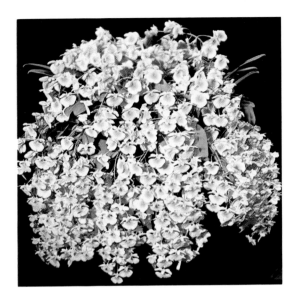

Dendrobium aggregatum
Jones and Scully, Inc.

Miltonia
Rod McLellan Co.

ANYONE FOR ORCHIDS?

↑　C. forbesii 'Marshall' CCM/AOS—86 pts

Exhibited by Ernest C. Marshall

A small species Cattleya grown to perfection

Photo by D. C. Flynn

Paphiopedilum rothschildianum →

A noble plant for the connoisseur

Catasetum detoideum
A collector's item

My own greenhouse is very bright and I seem to run it "dry." I'm still learning how to grow Masdevallias by getting some inexpensive and ordinary Pleurothallis. I'm trying them under the bench in the coolest wettest spot I have and they are potted in osmunda in clay pots. If they really "take off" I'll try those crazy Masdevallias again.

Whatever rare or odd thing you buy, you must give it all your attention and focus before it goes bad on you. A recent success for me is Tricoglottis phillippense var braciata. The person I bought it from said grow it high and dry. Well, his high and dry is not as high and dry as mine. In one week the plant had yellowed ever so slightly and the bottom leaves were a trifle wrinkled. I figured that even if it was vandaceous it simply couldn't take all that light. I moved it to below bench level and misted it every day. It recovered, grew and thrived. Every year, a month before it should set bud, I put it up in the brightest part of my greenhouse until I see the buds. Then it goes back to its own spot. We have a love affair, that plant and I.

Most of all, grow what you like. Don't buy something because it is expensive or famous or has snob appeal. Buy it because you like it. If you like it you'll look after it and it will like you back.

Phragmipedium schlimii 'Birchwood' AM/AOS
A real beauty for the connoisseur

ANYONE FOR ORCHIDS?

There are a few connoisseur plants that should be mentioned. Paphiopedilum rothschildianum and its hybrids will undoubtedly be of interest to collectors of fine plants. Paphiopedilum delanatii and its hybrids may possibly be of interest. Since Paphiopedilums have not been meristemmed commercially, the complex hybrids will continue to lure the collector. Some of the great parents to watch for in future seedlings are:

Beaute	F. C. Puddle
Winston Churchill	Souix
Danella	Erie
Paeony	Inca
Hellas	Gitana
Amanda	Gigi

Catasetum Gnomus 'Black River' CBM/AOS—81 pts
Exhibited by Black River Orchids, South Haven, Michigan
A collector's item

Phragmipedium caudatum var. Lindenii 'Birchwood'
CBM/AOS—81 pts
Exhibited by Dr. G. R. Clements
Pouchless—has great snob appeal

ANYONE FOR ORCHIDS?

The field of Cattleya hybrids Blc. Malworth 'Orchidglade' and Blc. Ports of Paradise 'Gleneyerie's Green Giant' FCC/AOS are certainly in the forefront.

I, for one, do not want to go into the fortune telling business. Which of the present trends will turn into the craze of the future, only the avid collector can say. At the moment, Equitant Oncidium hybrids are the rage. Brassavola nodosa crosses are starting to come on the market again after a certain amount of neglect. One thing is for sure, if the color of the flower is elusive that is the very color that everyone will want. Just keep in mind that today's rarity is tomorrow's commonplace.

X I
Cool Growers

In this period of energy shortage, some hobbyists are turning down their thermostats and turning to cool growers.

Most of these plants will do well in areas of the country where summers are not overly hot and steamy.

In the early days of orchid growing greenhousemen placed tropical orchids in what they called a "stove house." They believed, erroneously, that all orchids lived in a super saturated, hot, steamy environment. Needless to say the poor orchids perished with alarming rapidity. Eventually it was discovered that many orchids come from high elevations thriving in cloud swept eyries.

With today's technology and some ingenuity you can improvise a habitat for cool growing orchids unless you live in the most southern climes. Summer heat is the great enemy of these cool species but if you maintain a program of humidification, misting, shading and air conditioning, you can make it. The great benefit, of course, is saving on your heating bills.

Those of you who live in coastal California can naturalize these orchids on your grounds. They can be attached to trees, grown on driftwood or in baskets.

The following plants are tolerant of rather cold temperatures surviving even a few degrees of frost if out of doors.

Naturally, they will flourish in the protection of a cool greenhouse. Beward that plants grown in a moist greenhouse at 45° or 50° will be subject to botritis molds. This can be avoided by lots of moving air and less moisture in the air.

Ada aurantiaca 7-10 bright red flowers approximately 1 inch on a spike. Spring, semi-shade.

Epidendrum aromaticum very long branching sprays. Small flowers. Late spring.

Epidendrum cochleatum cockle shell upside down flower, almost ever blooming. Easy grower.

179

Epidendrum conopseum miniature loads of small greenish flowers. Various blooming time.

Epidendrum mariae (Encyclia mariae) the loveliest green flower with big white lip two or three to a spike. Summer.

Epidendrum nemorale spray of eight or ten pink flowers per spike. Summer.

Epidendrum prismatocarpum great for California out of doors. Nice yellow barred flowers. Various.

Epidendrum vitellinum bright red flowers with touch of yellow. Many to a spike. Summer.

Laelia albida 6-8 nice white two inch flowers on a spray. Fall.

Laelia anceps resembles a cattleya. Lavender or white varieties. Sprays of three or four big blooms. Winter.

Laelia autumnalis long flower spikes of lavender or white. Five to eight flowers. Fragrant. Fall.

Laelia pumila small plant with big bright blooms resembling a cattleya. Summer and fall.

Cattleya citrina (Encyclia citrina) lovely butter yellow blooms up to 4 inches. Grows on driftwood. Flowers pendulous. Summer, semi-sun.

Cochlioda sanquinea small bright pink flowers in a descending spike. Summer.

Coelogne cristata masses of glistening white flower racemes. Long lasting. The fat bulbs look like juicy water chestnuts.

Coelogne massangeana long chains of pendulous blooms, creamy with chocolate lip.

Coelogne ochracea not a big plant. Charming white flowers with rich red and yellow lip. Spring.

Dendrobium falcostrum short canes about 6 inch white flowers borne from the top of bulbs in profusion. Extremely hardy.

Dendrobium kingianum a charming small plant with lovely spikes of small lavender flowers. Easy grower, makes a nice specimen. Spring.

Dendrobium linguiforme creeping habit with lovely sprays of white flowers charming mounted on a totem or a tree fern monkey. Very hardy. Summer.

Dendrobium speciosum very showy profusely blooming 1 inch white flowers. Likes high light.

Epidendrum alatum sprays of 1 inch starry brownish flowers. Easy to grow. Summer.

Dendrobium nobile alba 'Stella Beals' CCM/AOS
Timber Tree Orchids

ANYONE FOR ORCHIDS?

Laelia majalis sturdy plant with large, showy blooms. Extremely hardy. Various.

Lycaste aromatica golden yellow flowers. Spring blooming. Shade.

Lycaste cruenta lovely golden flowers. Lip marked with red. Spring. Shade.

Lycaste deppi pale greenish sepal. Yellow lip. Summer. Shade.

Masdevallia caudata small plant. Two to three inches tall. Triangular flowers with thread like sepal. Lilac pink. Spring. Shade. Moist.

Masdevallia coccinea small plant with big two inch flowers. Bright magenta flowers. Various. Shade.

Masdevallia coriacea rather tubular shaped flower. Creamy white with red very floriferous flowers borne above. Leathery foliage. Summer.

Masdevallia cucullata four inch rich mahogany red flowers. Free blooming. Various.

Masdevallia elephanticeps blooms from base of plant. Spectacular exotic flower, yellow, brown and red. Summer.

Masdevallia erythrochaete long thread like tips of sepals. Rich dark red. Various.

Masdevallia militaris small plant with orange red flowers. Various.

Masdevallia rolfeana profuse oxblood blooms on short spikes. Summer.

Masdevallia veitchiana very large brilliant orange overlaid by blue irridescent. Summer and various.

Maxillaria lepidota three inch yellow brown blooms borne on six inch spikes from base of plant. Various.

Miltonia spectabilis very showy purple or white flowers. Several flowers on.

Odontoglossum apterum showy white blooms with brown barring and spotting. Six or more per spike. Easy grower. Winter. Spring.

Odontoglossum bictoniense upright spikes. Many greenish flowers with chestnut bars. Very easy grower. Spring.

Odontoglossum carniferum a long branched bloom spike to two feet long. Not ideal for a small greenhouse but great outdoors in California. Sepals and petals barred. Chestnut brown white lip.

Odontoglossum cervantisii charming dwarf plant with concentric markings on two inch white flowers borne four to five on a spray. Summer.

Odontoglossum citrosmum (pendulum) long lasting delicate pink two inch blooms on graceful pendulous spike. Summer to fall.

Odontoglossum cordatum a long eighteen spike with up to twelve star shaped warm brown flowers. Summer.

Odontoglossum grande king of the odonts. Big bold four to five inch flowers. Yellow with mahogany bars. Fall.

Odontoglossum insleayii tall sprays of eight to ten flowers yellow with brown barring. Three to four inch. Spring.

Odontoglossum laeve great for out of doors in California. Long spray. Vigorous grower. Pink lip. Spring.

Odontoglossum maculatum nice medium size plant with three inch yellow and brown barred flowers.

Odontoglossum pulchellum queen of the odonts. A small grower called Lily of the Valley Orchid. Lovely wax white flowers on a spray. Very easy to grow. Tolerant of almost any conditions. Spring.

Odontoglossum rossii white or pink flowers with brown barring. Two to four to a spike. Smallish plant. Summer.

Oncidium cavendishianum very showy spike two to three feet high with yellow and red spotted twisted sepals and a bright yellow lip.

Oncidium crispum large rich brown flowers on tall spikes eighteen inches to two feet high.

Oncidium excavatum great for outdoors. Three foot branching spikes of bright yellow and brown barred flowers.

Oncidium flexuosum smallish plant. Many tiny bright yellow flowers on a flexible spike.

Oncidium forbesii choice very showy, many brown and yellow flowers on an eighteen inch branching spike.

Oncidium incurvum small fragrant rose pink flowers on long sprays.

Oncidium lamelligerum spectacular giant spikes to twelve foot long. Not for small greenhouses but fabulous out of doors.

Oncidium leucochilum another super plant for out doors. Four to eight foot spikes branched and arching with many flowers. Sepals yellowish green barred with dark brown and a lovely white lip.

Photo by Lewis Ellsworth

Pleurothallis gelida var. Elvena CCM/AOS—84 pts
A marvelous miniature

Oncidium macranthum queen of the oncidiums. Three inch brown and gold flowers very full and round on a twining four to ten foot spike. Another biggie for out of doors.

Oncidium ornithorhyncum perfect for the small greenhouse. Cool or intermediate. Lovely lacy spikes of complex pink flowers. A charmer.

Oncidium tigrinum spectacular two inch flowers with broad yellow lip and tiger striped sepals ten or more to a spike.

Oncidium unicorne very hardy species from Brazil. Small dainty plant with greenish yellow flowers.

Paphiopedilums particularly green foliage types will do well in a shady spot in a California garden.

Pleione formosana deciduous bulbs sending up a lovely lavender Cattleya type flower in early spring. Similar and also desirable are *Pleione hookeriana, Pleione humilis, Pleione macalata* and *Pleione praecox.*

Pleurothallis these charming terrestrials from high elevations in Central and South America can be put in a rock garden situation and are equally at home in a cool greenhouse. Many are almost everblooming with tiny jewel like flowers.

Restrepia another group of miniatures for greenhouse or garden bearing exotic flowers resembling delicate insects. Charmers all.

Sobralias not for a greenhouse. Very tall foliage resembling bamboo. Lovely single Cattleya like flowers emerging over a long period.

Stanhopea tigrina a weird and wonderfully fragrant short lasting flower that comes out from the bottom of a moss lined basket.

Vanda cristata one of the few vandas that stands really cool outdoor conditions. Funny green blooms along the monopodial stem.

Zygopetalum mackayi good sized plant with striking greenish brown flowers with a gorgeous big violet and white lip on a two foot high spike. Very fragrant.

X I I
Original Habitats

Orchids are found everywhere in the world except the Polar regions and deserts. Knowing where an orchid comes from is a clue to its cultural needs. If you like to travel, you may include visiting orchid habitats on your trips.

Here is a list giving some general idea of where you may find certain orchid genera. Some are quite specific but there is a great deal of overlapping. Therefore, you may see a generic name appear on more than one list.

North America

Aplectrum	Goodyera
Arethusa	Habenaria
Calopogon	Ibidium
Calypso	Liparis
Cephalanthera	Oncidium
Cypripedium	Orchis
Cyrtopodium	Pogonia
Epidendrum	Spiranthes
Epipactis	

South America

Anguloa	Leptotes
Bifrenaria	Lockhartia
Brassavola	Lycaste
Brassia	Masdevalia
Catasetum	Maxillaria
Cattleya	Miltonia
Cochlioda	Mormodes
Cycnoches	Odontoglossum
Chondrorhyncha	Oncidium
Epidendrum	Peristeria
Gongora	Pleurothallis
Huntleya	Phragmipedium
Laelia	Rodriguezia

Schomburgkia
Sobralia
Stanhopea

Trichopilia
Vanilla
Warscewiczella
Zygopetalum

Mexico and the Indies

Anguloa
Brassavola
Brassia
Broughtonia
Catasetum
Cattleya
Chysis
Cycnoches
Chondrorhyncha
Diacrium
Epidendrum
Gongora
Huntleya
Laelia
Lockhartia

Lycaste
Masdevallia
Miltonia
Mormodes
Odontoglossum
Peristeria
Pleurothallis
Phragmipedium
Rodriquezia
Schomburgkia
Sobralia
Stanhopea
Trichopilia
Vanilla
Warscewiczilla

Europe

Arachnites
Bletilla
Cephalanthera
Corallorhiza
Cypripedium
Epipactus
Goodyera
Gymnadenia

Habenaria
Herminum
Limodorum
Liparis
Listera
Orchis
Neotina
Spiranthes

Africa and Madagascar

Aerangis
Aeranthes
Angraecum
Ansellia
Bulbophyllum
Cymbidiella
Cynorchis
Corymbis
Disa
Eulophia

Eulophidium
Eulophiella
Gastrorchis
Habenaria
Lissochilus
Megaclinium
Polytachya
Satyrium
Stenoglottis
Vanilla

ANYONE FOR ORCHIDS?

Australia

Bulbophyllum
Calandenia
Calanthe
Caleana
Cymbidium
Dendrobium
Diuris
Drakaea
Earina
Eulophia

Liparis
Malaxis
Oberonia
Phaius
Phreatia
Pyerostylis
Sarcochilis
Rhinerrhiza
Thelymitra

Asia

Ascocentrum
Bulbophyllum
Calanthe
Cyperorchis
Cirrhopetalum
Coelogyne
Cymbidium
Dendrobium

Eulophia
Gastrochilis
Kingiella
Paphiopedilum
Pleione
Renanthera
Thunia
Vanda

*Malay Peninsula, Philippines, Indonesia
and Pacific Islands*

Acampe
Aerides
Arachnis
Ascocentrum
Calanthe
Cirrhopetalum
Coelogyne
Dendrobium
Dendrochilium
Grammatophyllum
Kingiella

Paphiopedilum
Phalaenopsis
Phaius
Pholidota
Pleione
Renanthera
Rhynchostylis
Saccolabium
Spathoglottis
Thunia
Vanda

XIII
Glossary

GLOSSARY OF ORCHID NAMES, excerpted from *An Orchidist's Glossary,* published by the American Orchid Society.

The Generic Names of Orchids

A

Acacallis (a-ka-kall'-iss). A genus related to *Zygopetalum,* described by Lindley in 1853 and dedicated to a Greek nymph.

Acampe (a-kam'-pe). A small genus of tropical Asian and African orchids, related to *Vanda* and *Sarcanthus,* it was described by Lindley in 1853, the name derived from the Greek in reference to the brittle rigidity of the small flowers.

Ada (ay'-da). A genus of but two species from the Colombian Andes, allied to *Odontoglossum,* described by Lindley in 1853, the name referring to Ada, sister of Artimisia in Caria, an historical character.

Aerangis (ay-er-rang'-giss). A genus of African orchids related to *Angraceum,* established by Reichenbach in 1865, the name meaning "air vessel," probably in allusion to the long spur.

Aeranthes (ay-er-an'-theez). A genus of about thirty species of sarcanthine orchids, chiefly from Madagascar and adjacent islands, characterized by their complex flowers, the genus having been described by Lindley in 1824 and named in allusion to the epiphytic habit of the plants.

Aerides (air'-i-deez). A genus of vandaceous orchids from tropical Asia, established by Louirero in 1790, the name alluding to their epiphytic habit.

Angraecum (an-grye'-kum). A genus of Asiatic vandaceous orchids centered mainly in Africa and Madagascar, the name being Latinized from the Malay *Angurek* which refers to all epiphytic orchids of similar habit; it was established by Bory in 1804.

Anguloa (an-gyew-loh'-a). A small genus of orchids from the Andean regions, allied to *Lycaste,* it was named in 1794 by Ruiz and Pavon in honor of Don Francisco de Angulo, Director of Mines in Peru.

Ansellia (an-sell'-ee-a). A small genus of epiphytic or lithophytic orchids from tropical Africa, named by Lindley in 1844 in honor of John Ansell, English botanist of the Royal Hortitural Society's Chiswick Gardens.

Arachnis (a-rack'-niss). A small genus of tropical Asiatic orchids related to *Vanda,* named by Blume in 1825 in reference to the spiderlike flowers.

Ascocentrum (ass-koh-sen'-trum). A small genus of compact-growing monopodial orchids from Southeast Asia and the Malayan Archipelago, allied to *Vanda,* it was described by Schlechter in 1913, the name referring to the bag-like spur at the base of the lip.

Aspasia (a-spay'-zi-a). A small genus in the *Oncidium* alliance, described by Lindley in 1832, the name in tribute to Aspasia, wife of Pericles.

B

Batemannia (bayt-man'-nee-a). A very small genus of epiphytic orchids from northern South America, closely related to *Zygopetalum, Zygosepalum* and *Promenaea,* it was founded in 1834 by Lindley in compliment to James Bateman, an ardent grower and collector of orchids and known for his books "Orchids of Mexico and Guatemala" and "A Monograph of Odontoglossum."

Bifrenaria (bye-fren-air'-i-a). A genus of orchids related to *Lycaste,* from Central and South America, described by Lindley in 1833, the name alluding to the two caudicles on the pollinia.

Bletia (blee'-shia). A sizable genus of American terrestrial orchids related to *Phaius* and *Spathoglottis,* described by Ruiz and Pavon in 1794 in honor of Don Luis Blet, a Spanish apothecary of the 18th century who maintained a botanic garden in Algeciras.

Bletilla (ble-till'-a). A small genus of terrestrial orchids from the region embracing China, Japan and Formosa, allied to the

American genera of *Arethusa* and *Calopogon,* it was described by Reichenbach in 1853, the name implying its resemblance to the genus *Bletia,* with which it is only distantly related.

Bollea (boh'-lee-a). A small genus of high-altitude South American epiphytic orchids, allied to *Huntleya* and *Cochleanthes,* it was described by Riechenbach in 1852, being dedicated to Dr. Karl Bolle, a German patron of horticulture.

Brassavola (bra-sah'-voh-la). A genus of tropical American orchids closely allied to *Cattleya* and *Laelia,* described by Robert Brown in 1813 and dedicated to Sr. Antonio Musa Brasavola, a Venetian nobleman and botanist.

Brassia (brass'-ee-a). A genus in the *Oncidium* alliance characterized by spider-like flowers, described by Robert Brown in 1813 in honor of William Brass, an 18th-century botanical illustrator.

Broughtonia (brow-toh'-nee-a). A monotypic genus of attractive epiphytic orchids from the island of Jamaica, related to *Laelia* and *Cattleya,* it was established by Robert Brown in 1813, being dedicated to Arthur Broughton, an English botanist who worked in Jamaica in the early 19th century.

Bulbophyllum (bulb-oh-fill'-um). An extremely large genus of orchids, primarily Asiatic, described by du Petit-Thouars in 1822, the name referring to the fleshy leaves borne singly on prominent pseudobulbs.

C

Calanthe (kal-an'-thee). A large genus of terrestrial or semi-epiphytic orchids primarily from Africa, tropical Asia, Australia and the Pacific Islands, related to *Phaius,* it was described by Robert Brown in 1821, the name derived from the Greek meaning "beautiful flower." One species, *Calanthe mexicana,* is found in the New World.

Camplyocentrum (kam-pyr-loh-sen'-trum). A sizable genus of epiphytic orchids from tropical America, especially Brazil, notable fro the many species which have no leaves, it was established in 1881, the name derived from the Greek and meaning "crooked spur" in reference to the slender and sharply curved spur of the lip.

Catasetum (kat-a-see'-tum). A large genus of chiefly epiphytic orchids from tropical America, allied to *Mormodes* and *Cycnoches,* it was established by L. C. Richard in 1822, the name derived from the Greek and referring to the antenna-like processes of the column of the strangely shaped flowers.

Cattleya (kat'-lee-a). A tropical American genus of showy-flowered epiphytic orchids related to *Epidendrum, Laelia* and *Brassavola,* it was founded by Lindley in 1824 and dedicated by him to William Cattley, of Barnet, England, an ardent horticulturist and patron of botany.

Cattleyopsis (kat-lee-op'-siss). A very small genus of dwarf epiphytes from the Antilles, especially Cuba, allied to *Broughtonia* and *Laeliopsis,* it was described by Lemaire in 1853, the name indicating the resemblance of the flowers to those of the genus *Cattleya.*

Cochleanthes (kok-lee-an'-theez). A small genus of tropical American epiphytic orchids, related to *Chondrorhyncha,* containing species until recently ascribed to *Warscewiczella, Warrea, Zygopetalum* and allied genera, the genus being established by Rafinesque in 1836, the name alluding to the shell-like character of the flowers of the type species, described earlier in 1836 as *Zygopeatlum cochleare* by Lindley.

Cochlioda (kok-lee-oh'-da). A very small genus of epiphytic Andean orchids in the *Oncidium* alliance, it was described by Lindley in 1853, the name suggested by the shell-like calluses on the lip.

Coelogyne (see-loj'-in-ee). A large genus of chiefly epiphytic orchids from tropical Asia, described by Lindley in 1822, the name suggesting the deeply excavated stigma.

Colax (koh'-laks). A very small genus of epiphytic orchids from Brazil, closely allied to *Zygopetalum,* it was established by Lindley in 1826, the name being Greek and meaning parasite, in reference to the epiphytic habit of the plants.

Coryanthes (ko-ree-an'-theez). A small genus of epiphytic orchids with extraordinary flowers from the American tropics, related to *Stanhopea* and *Gongora,* it was described by Hooker in 1831, the name derived from the Greek meaning "helmet flower" in reference to the helmet-shaped epichile of the lip.

Cycnoches (sik'-no-keez). A small genus of tropical American epiphytic orchids, related to *Catasetum* and *Mormodes* and described by Lindley in 1832, it is popularly known as the

"Swan Orchid," the generic name alluding to the gracefully arched column of the male flowers which is indeed swan-like.

Cymbidium (sim-bid'-ee-um). A sizable genus of horticulturally important orchids, found chiefly in the Indian Himalayas, it was established by Swartz in 1799, the name derived from the Greek in allusion to the boat-shaped lip.

Cypripedium (sip-ree-pee'-dee-um). Our common Lady's-slipper, a medium-sized genus of terrestrial orchids distributed in the north temperate zone of both hemispheres, it was described by Linnaeus in 1753, the name, incorrectly Latinized from the Greek meaning "Venus' scandal," refers to the slipper-like lip.

Cyrtopodium (sir-to-poh'-dee-um). A medium-sized genus of terrestrial or epiphytic orchids of tropical America, popularly called "Cow's-horn Orchids," described in 1813 by Robert Brown, the name referring to the upcurved column-foot.

Cyrtorchis (sir'-tor-kiss). A small genus of angraecoid orchids from tropical Africa, primarily epiphytic, it was described by Schlechter in 1914, the name probably alluding to the fleshy character of the floral segments.

D

Dendrobium (den-droh'-bee-um). An extremely large genus of tropical Asian epiphytic orchids, very variable in plant structure, established by Swartz in 1799, the name derived from the Greek for tree and life, in reference to the epiphytic habit of the plants.

Dendrochilum (den-droh-kye'-lum). A large genus of Asiatic orchids related to *Coelogyne,* noted for the long arching scapes with many flowers, it was described by Blume in 1825, the name possibly referring to the epiphytic habit of the plants.

Dendrophylax (den-droh-fye'-laks). A very small genus of leafless monopodial orchids related to *Angraecum,* described in 1861 by Reichenbach, the name alluding to the manner in which the roots surround the tree branch on which the plant grows.

Dichaea (dye-kee'-a). A medium-sized genus of pseudomonopodial epiphytic orchids from tropical America, characterized by two ranks of short, flattened, closely set leaves, it was erected by Lindley in 1833, the name derived from the Greek meaning two-fold in reference to the two ranks of leaves.

Disa (dye'-sa). A very large genus of terrestrial orchids found chiefly in tropical and South Africa, established by Bergius in 1767, the derivation of the name being obscure, but the genus is noted for the beauty and unusual structure of its flowers.

Domingoa (doh-ming-goh'-a). A very small genus of epiphytic orchids from the West Indies, related to *Laelia,* established by Schlechter in 1913, the name derived from Santo Domingo, former name of the Dominican Republic from whence came the type species.

Doritis (doh-rye'-tis). A very small, possibly monotypic, genus of epiphytic vandaceous orchids, closely related to *Phalaenopsis,* sparsely distributed throughout Southeast Asia and Sumatra, it was described by Lindley in 1833, the name referring to Doritis, one of the names for the goddess Aphrodite.

E

Epidendrum (eh-pi-den'-drum). An extremely large genus of tropical American orchids closely related to *Laelia* and *Cattleya,* the generic name having been used by Linnaeus in 1753 in reference to the epiphytic habit of the plants and originally including a number of concepts now referred to different genera of epiphytic orchids.

Epigeneium (eh-pi-jee'-nee-um). A medium-sized genus of epiphytic orchids from the Asiatic tropics, related to *Dendrobium* and formerly placed in the genus *Sarcopodium,* it was established by Gagnepain in 1932, the name meaning "upon the chin" and referring to the position of the petals and lateral sepals on the column-foot.

Epipactis (eh-pi-tak'-tis). A genus of circumboreal terrestrial orchids related to *Cephalanthera,* established in 1800 by Swartz who employed an ancient name originally used by Theophrastus (370–285 B.C.).

Eria (ear'-ee-a). A very large genus of Asiatic orchids closely related to *Dendrobium,* described in 1825 by Lindley, the name alluding to the woolly outer surface of the sepals and petals.

Eulophia (yew-loh'-fee-a). A very large genus of terrestrial orchids related to *Cyrtopodium,* widespread throughout the warm areas of the world but greatest in Central Africa, described in 1823 by Robert Brown, the name referring to the crest on the lip.

G

Galeandra (gal-ee-an'-dra). A small genus of epiphytic or terrestrial orchids from the American tropics, related to *Polystachya* and described by Lindley in 1830, the name referring to the helmet-shaped anther cap.

Gastorchis (gas-tork'-is). A small genus of semi-terrestrial orchids from Madagascar and the Mascarene Islands, related to *Phaius* and *Calanthe,* it was first proposed by du Petit-Thouars in 1822, the name referring to the basally inflated or saccate lip of the flowers.

Gastrochilus (gas-tro-kye'-lus). A small genus of Asiatic epiphytes from Japan, the Himalayas and Indonesia, related to *Sarcochilus,* it was described by D. Don in 1825, the name in allusion to the belly-shaped lip of the flowers in this genus.

Gomesa (go-mee'-sa). A genus of a dozen epiphytic species from Brazil, allied to *Oncidium,* it was established in 1815 by Robert Brown to commemorate Dr. Bernardino Antonio Gomes, a Portuguese naval physician and botanist author of a book on the medicinal plants of Brazil.

Gongora (gon-gor'-ah). A genus of about twenty-five species confined to the American tropics, the flowers of which are extremely corylicate and multicolored; related to *Stanhopea* and *Coryanthes,* it was described in 1794 by Ruiz and Pavon, and dedicated Don Antonio Cabellero y Gongora, Bishop of Cordova, Spain.

Grammatophyllum (gram-mat-o-fill'-um). A small genus of epiphytic orchids from Malaya, Indonesia or the Philippines, related to *Cymbidium* and noted for the large size of the plants, it was described in 1825 by Blume, the name possibly referring to the markings on the flowers or the prominent parallel leaf-veins.

ANYONE FOR ORCHIDS?

H

Habenaria (hab-en-ay'-ri-a). A very large genus of terrestrial orchids distributed throughout the world, it was described by Willdenow in 1805, the name derived from the Latin meaning rein, alluding to the strap-like divisions of the petals and lip.

Haemaria (hee-may'-ree-a). A monotypic genus of highly variable terrestrial orchids from tropical Asia, noted for its attractive foliage as one of the "Jewel Orchids," it was described by Lindley in 1826 but is now considered a synonym for the genus *Ludisia* (q.v.).

Hexisea (heks-iss'-ee-a). A small genus of epiphytic orchids from Middle America and northern South America, related to *Epidendrum,* it was described in 1834 by Lindley, the name derived from the fact that the six segments of the flower's perianth are about equal in size and shape.

Houlletia (hoo-let'-ee-a). A small tropical American genus of less than ten epiphytic species, allied to *Stanhopea,* it was described by Brongniart in 1841 and dedicated to Houllet (1811–1890), a French horticulturist and Assistant Curator at the Jardin des Plantes, Paris, who collected the type species in Brazil.

Huntleya (hunt'-lee-a). A small genus of epiphytic orchids from tropical America, allied to *Zygopetalum,* it was described by Bateman in 1837, the name complimenting the Rev. J. T. Huntley, an English orchid enthusiast of the nineteenth century.

I

Ionopsis (eye-o-nop'-siss). A small genus of tropical and subtropical American orchids, usually epiphytic, described in 1815 by Humboldt, Bonpland and Kunth, the name referring to the violet-like appearance of the flowers.

Isochilus (eye-so-kye'-lus). A very small genus of tropical American epiphytes allied to *Ponera,* described by Robert Brown in 1813, the name alluding to the fact that the lip is usually equal to the sepals in size.

J

Jumellea (joo-mell'-ee-a). A sizable genus of epiphytic orchids from Madagascar and tropical Africa, closely related to *Angraecum,* it was erected by Schlechter in 1914, and dedicated to Professor Henry Jumelle, a French botanist from Marseilles who investigated the flora of Madagascar in the late nineteenth century.

L

Laelia (lee'-lee-a; lye'-lee-a; lay'-lee-a). A large genus of showy epiphytic orchids from tropical America, related to *Cattleya* and *Epidendrum,* it was described by Lindley in 1831, the name obscure but possibly dedicated to Laelia, one of the Vestal Virgins.

Laeliopsis (lee-li-op'-siss). A small genus of epiphytic orchids from the West Indies, related to *Broughtonia,* it was established in 1853 by Lindley, the name alluding to the similarity of the species to the members of the genus *Laelia.*

Lepanthes (lee-pan'-theez). A large genus of small-flowered dwarf epiphytic orchids of tropical America, related to *Pleurothallis* and *Masdevallia,* it was founded by Swartz in 1799, the name referring to the tiny scale-like flowers.

Lepanthopsis (lee-pan-thop'-siss). A small genus of dwarf epiphytic orchids from tropical America, related to *Lepanthes* as its name implies, it was described by Oakes Ames in 1933.

Leptotes (lep-toh'-teez). A small genus of epiphytic orchids from Brazil and Paraguay, related to *Laelia,* it was described by Lindley in 1833, the name referring to the slender leaves.

Liparis (lip'-a-riss). A very large genus of terrestrial to epiphytic orchids found mostly in tropical Asia but scattered worldwide; somewhat related to *Malaxis,* it was established in 1818 by L. C. Richard, the name derived from the Greek word meaning fat or greasy, in reference to the shining surface of the leaves of many of the species.

Lockhartia (lok-hart'-ee-a). A moderately large genus of epiphytic orchids from the American tropics, related to *Oncidium* and commonly called the "Braided Orchid" because of the character of the arrangement of the leaves, it was described in 1827 by Hooker in compliment to David Lockhart.

Lycaste (lye-kass'-tee). A moderately sized genus of about twenty-five species of epiphytic, or semi-terrestrial orchids of tropical America, described by Lindley in 1843 and dedicated to the beautiful daughter of Priam, last king of Troy.

M

Masdevallia (maz-de-val'-lee-a). A large genus of epiphytic orchids from tropical America, related to *Pleurothallis,* it was established in 1794 by Ruiz and Pavon, the name complimenting Dr. Jose Masdevall, a Spanish physician and botanist of the 18th century.

Maxillaria (mak-sil-lair'-ee-a). A large genus of chiefly epiphytic orchids from the American tropics, related to *Scuticaria* and *Trigonidium,* it was described by Ruiz and Pavon in 1794, the name alluding to the fancied resemblance of the flowers to the jaws of an insect.

Meiracyllium (mye-ra-sill'-ee-um). A very small genus of two species of epiphytic or lithophytic orchids from Mexico and Guatemala, allied to *Laelia,* founded by Reicherbach in 1864, the name referring to the dwarf, creeping habit of the plants.

Miltonia (mil-toh'-nee-a). A medium-sized genus of epiphytic orchids from Central and South America belonging to the *Oncidium* alliance, it was described in 1837 by Lindley who dedicated it to the Earl Fitzwilliam, Viscount Milton (1748–1833), a patron of horticulture.

Mormodes (mor-mor'-deez). A small genus of about twenty species of epiphytic or semi-terrestrial orchids from tropical America, allied to *Catasetum* and *Cycnoches,* it was described by Lindley in 1836, the name alluding to the strange appearance of the flowers.

N

Nageliella (nay'-gel-i-ell'-a). A very small genus of Middle American orchids, related to *Epidendrum* and *Scaphyglottis,* it was established in 1940 by Louis O. Williams, the name honoring the contemporary collector of Mexican orchids, Herr Otto Nagel.

Neofinetia (nee-o-fin-ay'-tee-a). A monotypic genus of epiphytic orchids from Japan, related to *Angraecum,* it was established by Hu in 1925 and dedicated to M. Achille Finet, a French botanist who worked on the orchids of China and Japan.

Notylia (no-till'-ee-a). A medium-sized genus of compact, small-flowered epiphytic or lithophytic orchids from tropical America, it was established by Lindley in 1825, the name, meaning "humpback," alluding to an unusual hump or callosity on the stigma.

O

Octomeria (ok-toh-may'-ree-a). A rather small genus of epiphytic orchids from the American tropics, related to *Pleurothallis,* it was described in 1813 by Robert Brown, the name alluding to the eight pollinia.

Odontoglossum (o-don-toh-gloss'-um). A very large genus of epiphytic orchids from tropical America belonging to the *Oncidium* alliance, it was established by Humboldt, Bonpland and Kunth in 1815, the name referring to the toothed crest on the lip of most of the species.

Oncidium (on-sid'-ee-um). A very large genus of epiphytic orchids from tropical America, it was founded by Swartz in 1800, the name alluding to the warty callus on the lip of the species in the genus.

Ornithocephalus (or-nith-o-seff'-al-us). A small genus of pseudobulbless epiphytes from the American tropics, related to *Phymatidium* and *Zygostates,* it was established by Hooker in 1825, the name alluding to the resemblance of the column and anther to the head of a bird.

P

Paphiopedilum (paff-i-e-pee'-di-lum). A sizable genus of the Lady's-slipper orchids from the Asiatic tropics, formerly included in the genus *Cypripedium,* the name having been proposed by Pfitzer in 1886 in allusion to the slipper-shaped lip.

Peristeria (pare-i-stare'-ee-a). A small genus of epiphytic orchids from Panama and northern South America, related to *Gongora,* it was described by Hooker in 1831, the name meaning "little dove" from the resemblance of the column and lip to a dove. *Peristeria elata* is popularly called the "Dove Orchid."

Pescatoria (pess-ka-tor'-i-a). A small genus of pseudobulbless epiphytic orchids, distributed from Costa Rica to Ecuador, it is related to *Huntleya* and was described in 1852 by Reichenbach who dedicated it to M. Pescatore, a French orchid enthusiast.

Phaius (fay'-us). A medium-sized genus of semiterrestrial orchids widely distributed in Indo-Malaysia and China, related to *Calanthe* and *Spathoglottis,* it was described by Loureiro in 1790, the name referring to the swarthy colors of the flowers.

Phalaenopsis (fal-en-op'-siss). A sizable genus of showy epiphytic orchids from the Asiatic tropics, related to *Rhynchostylis* and *Vanda,* it was founded by Blume in 1825, the name referring to the moth-like appearance of the flowers.

Pholidota (foh-li-doh'-ta). A medium-sized genus of pseudobulbous epiphytes from India and southern China to Australia, related to *Dendrochilum* and *Coelogyne,* it was established in 1825 by Lindley, the name arising from the presence of scaly bracts on the inflorescence and from which came the common name of "Rattlesnake Orchid."

Phragmipedium (frag-mi-pee'-di-um). A small genus of Lady's slipper orchids distributed from Costa Rica to Peru, the genus was established by Rolfe in 1896; related to *Cypripedium,* in cultivation plants of this genus have incorrectly been called *Selenipedium.*

Physosiphon (fye-zoss'-i-fon). A small genus of tufted epiphytic orchids from the American tropics, related to *Pleurothallis* and *Stelis,* it was founded by Lindley in 1836, the name referring to the tube-like base of the connate sepals.

Pleione (plye-oh'-nee). A small genus of pseudobulbous orchids from the Himalayas and Southeast Asia, related to *Coelogyne,* it was established in 1825 by D. Don who dedicated it to Pleione, mother of the Pleiades in Greek mythology.

Pleurothallis (plur-o-thal'-liss). An extremely large genus of chiefly epiphytic pseudobulbous orchids from the American Tropics, related to *Masdevallia* and *Stelis,* it was established in 1813 by Robert Brown, the name referring to the riblike leaf stalks found in most species.

Pogonia (poh-goh'-nee-a). A small genus of terrestrial orchids widely distributed in the North Temperate Zone in both hemispheres, it was founded by Jussieu in 1789, the name referring to the bearded crest on the lip of most species.

Polyrrhiza (pol-ee-rye'-za). A very small genus of leafless epiphytic orchids found in the tropics and subtropics of South Florida and the Caribbean area, it is related to *Dendrophylax* and *Camphylocentrum;* it was described by Pfitzer in 1889, the name referring to the many conspicuous roots.

Promenaea (pro-men-ee'-a). A small genus of dwarf epiphytic orchids from Brazil and neighboring areas, related to *Zygopetalum,* it was described by Lindley in 1843, the name derived from Promeneia, a priestess at Dodona.

R

Renanthera (ren-ann'-ther-a). A small genus of primarily epiphytic orchids, distributed from southeast Asia through Malaysia and the Philippines, it is related to *Vanda* and *Arachnis;* it was established in 1790 by Loureiro, the name alluding to the kidney-shaped anthers of the flowers.

Rhynchostylis (rink-oh-stye'-liss; rin-kos'-ti-liss). A very small genus of four species of epiphytic orchids, widely distributed from India and Ceylon through Burma, Indo-China and Malaysia to the Philippines, it is related to *Aerides* and *Vanda;* it was first described by Blume in 1825 the name alluding to the beaked column of the type species.

Rodriguezia (roh-dri-geez'-ee-a; rod-ri-gay'-zi-a). A small genus of epiphytic orchids in South America, extending into Central America, related to *Ionopsis* and established in 1794 by Ruiz and Pavon, commemorating the 18th-century Spanish botanist and apothecary, Don Manuel Rodriguez.

S

Saccolabium (sak-ko-lay'-bee-um). A small genus of small-flowered epiphytic orchids of Southeast Asia, related to *Vanda* and *Ascocentrum,* it was established by Blume in 1825, the name alluding to the bag-like shape of the lip; uncommon in cultivation, it has been confused with *Rhynchostylis, Sarcanthus* and other genera.

Schomburgkia (shom-berg'-kee-a). A small genus of epiphytic orchids from the American tropics and subtropics, often included in the genus *Laelia* to which it is closely allied, it was established in 1838 by Lindley who dedicated it to the German botanist, Sir Robert Schomburgk (1804–1865).

Selenipedium (se-lee-ni-pee'-dee-um). A very small genus of South American terrestrial orchids related to *Cypripedium*, it was described in 1854 by Reichenbach, the name referring to Selene, the goddess of the moon in Greek mythology.

Sigmatostalix (sig-mat-o-stay'-liks). A small genus of tropical American epiphytic orchids found from Mexico to Brazil, it is related to *Oncidium;* described in 1852 by Reichenbach, the name alludes to the sigmoid or s-shaped appearance of the column and lip.

Sobralia (so-bral'-ee-a). A distinctive genus of terrestrial and lithophytic orchids from Mexico, Central and South America, it is characterized by its reed-like stems, plicate leaves and *Cattleya*-like flowers; it was founded in 1794 by Ruiz and Pavon in honor of the Spanish physician, Dr. Francisco Sobral.

Sophronitis (sof-roh-nye'-tiss). A small genus of dwarf epiphytic orchids from Brazil, related to *Laelia* and *Cattleya,* it was described by Lindley in 1824, the name alluding to the modest size of the plants.

Spathoglottis (spath-oh-glot'-tiss). A medium-sized genus of terrestrial orchids distributed from northern India and southern China through Malaysia and the Philippines into Australia and New Caledonia, it is allied to *Calanthe* and *Phaius;* described by Blume in 1825, the name alludes to the lip of the flowers.

Stanhopea (stan-hope'-ee-a). A medium-sized genus of epiphytic orchids from the American tropics, related to *Gongora* and *Coryanthes,* described by Frost in 1829, the name honoring the Right Honorable Philip Henry, fourth Earl of Stanhope, then just elected President of the London Medico-Botanical Society.

Stelis (stee'-lis). A very large genus of minute-flowered epiphytic orchids from the American tropics and subtropics related to *Pleurothallis* and *Masdevallia,* it was established in 1899 by Swartz, the name alluding indirectly to the epiphytic habit of the genus.

T

Telipogon (tel-i-poh'-gun). A medium-sized genus of tropical American dwarf epiphytic orchids found in the high cloud forests from Costa Rica to Peru, it was established by Humboldt, Bonpland and Kunth in 1815, the name descriptive of the bearded column.

Thunia (too'-nee-a). A small genus of terrestrial and semiterrestrial orchids from the mountains of northeast India and Burma to Malaya, related to *Arundina,* it was named by Reichenbach in 1852 in honor of Count von Thun Hohenstein of Tetschin, Bohemia.

Trichocentrum (trik-o-sen'-trum). A small genus of dwarf epiphytic orchids, distributed from Mexico to Brazil and Peru, it is related to *Ionopsis* and *Comparettia,* the name applied in 1837 by Poeppig and Endlicher, referring to the long, slender spur of the flowers of most species.

Trichoglottis (trik-o-glott'-iss). A medium-sized genus of vandaceous orchids from southeast Asia, Malaysia and the Philippines, it was established by Blume in 1825, the name referring to the pubescence on the lip of the flowers.

Trichopilia (trik-o-pill'-ia). A medium-sized genus of rather showy pseudobulbous orchids distributed from Mexico to Bolivia and Brazil, it was described in 1836 by Lindley, the name derived from the fringed margin of the column.

Trigonidium (trig-o nid'-ee-um). A small genus of epiphytic orchids which range from Mexico to Brazil, related to *Maxillaria,* it was described in 1837 by Lindley who derived the name from the triangular form of several parts of the flowers.

V

Vanda (van'-da). A sizable genus of showy epiphytic orchids of monopodial habit, found in the Asiatic tropics, it was described by Jones in 1795, the name being derived from the Sanskrit for epiphyte.

Vandopsis (van-dop'-siss). A small genus of vandaceous orchids, distributed from Burma and Siam to the Philippines and New Guinea, closely allied to *Trichoglottis,* it was described in 1889 by Pfitzer, the name implying a resemblance to *Vanda.*

Vanilla (va-nil'-la). A large genus of vinelike orchids, widely distributed in the tropics and subtropics of both hemispheres, it is related to *Pogonia;* described in 1799 by Swartz, the name is derived from the Spanish *vainilla,* meaning "little pod," and refers to the slender pod-like fruit.

W

Warscewiczella (war-se-wik-zell'-a). A former name for a small group of tropical American epiphytic orchids now referred to the genus *Cochleanthes,* it was described by Reichenbach in 1852 in honor of the Polish botanist Dr. Josef Warsewicz (1812–1866) who collected in Middle and South America.

X

Xylobium (zye-loh'-bee-um). A small genus of pseudobulbous epiphytic orchids from Central and South America, related to *Bifrenaria* and *Lycaste,* it was established by Lindley in 1825, the name referring to the epiphytic habit of the species.

Z

Zygopetalum (zye-go-pet'-a-lum). A varyingly defined genus of terrestrial to epiphytic orchids distributed throughout northern South America and north to Mexico, it is related to *Colax* and *Promenaea,* having been founded by Hooker in 1827, the name referring to the yoke-like callus on the base of the lip.

Zygosepalum (zye-go-sep'-a-lum). A very small genus of handsome epiphytic orchids from northern South America, formerly known as *Menadenium,* it was founded by Reichenbach in 1803, the name referring to the sepals which are basally connate.

The Species Names of Orchids

A

abbreviatus, -a, -um (a-bree-vee-ay'-tus). Shortened; abbreviated.

acaulis, -e (a-kaw'-lis). Having no stem, or only a very short stem.

acicularis, -e (a-sik-yew-lair'-is). Pointed; needle-like.

acinaciformis, -e (a-sin-a-si-form'-is). Shaped like a curved sword or scimitar.

acklandiae (ak-klan'-dee-eye). In compliment to the late Lady Ackland, wife of Sir Thomas D. Ackland, of Killerton, near Exeter, by whom the *Cattleya* so named was introduced from Brazil.

acuminatus, -a, -um (ak-yew-min-ay'-tus). Tapering into a long narrow point; acuminate.

aemulus, -a, -um (eye'-mew-lus). Rivaling; hence superior, very handsome.

africanus, -a, -um (af-rik-kay'-nus). Native of Africa; African.

aggregatus, -a, -um (ag-greg-gay'-tus). Clustered in a dense mass; aggregate.

alatus, -a, -um (al-ay'-tus). Winged; having wings or winglike parts; alate.

alba or *album* (al'-buh, al'-bum). White; a white or pale phase of a species or hybrid whose flowers normally are colored, but usually retaining some yellow or green pigment, particularly in the throat.

albescens (al-bess'senz). Whitish; becoming white.

albidofulvus, -a, -um (al-bid-o-full'-vus). Yellow and white.

albidus, -a, -um (al'-bid-us). Whitish.

albostriatus, -a, -um (al-bo-strye-ay'-tus). Striped with white.

albus, -a, -um (al'-bus). Clear, but not shining, white.

altissimus, -a, -um (al-tiss'-ee-mus). Very tall, or tallest of its congeners.

altus, -a, -um (al'-tus). Tall.

amabilis, -e (a-mah'-bill-iss). Lovely.

ambiguus, -a, -um (am-big'-yew-us). Doubtful, uncertain; ambiguous.

amboinensis, -e (am-boy-nen'-sis). Native to the island of Amboina in the Malayan archipelago.

amethystinus, -a, -um (am-eh-this-tye'-nus). Pale violet in color.

amethystoglossus, -a, -um (am-e-this-toh-gloss'-us). Having an amethyst-colored lip.

amoenus -a, -um (am-een'-us). Charming; delightful.

ampliatus, -a, -um (am-pli-ay'-tus). Enlarged.

amplus, -a, -um (am'-plus). Large and thus fine, noble.

ampullaceus, -a, -um (am-pew-lay'-see-us). Flask or bottle-shaped.

anceps (an'-seps). Two-edged, such as in a flattened stem.

angustifolius, -a, -um (an-gus-ti-foh'-lee-us). Having narrow leaves.

antenniferus, -a, -um (an-ten-if'-fer-us). Bearing antennae.

apiatus, -a, -um (a-pee-ay'-tus). Bee-like.

apiculatus, -a, -um (a-pik-yew-lay'-tus). Ending abruptly in a short sharp point; apiculate.

appendiculatus, -a, -um (a-pen-dik-yew-lay'-tus). Having appendages, such as a crest, hairs, etc.

argenteus, -a -um (ar-jen'-tee-us). Silvery.

armeniacus, -a, -um (ar-men-i-ay'-kus). Apricot-colored.

aromaticus, -a, -um (a-ro-mat'-ik-us). Fragrant; aromatic.

ascendens (a-sen'-denz). Rising somewhat obliquely or curving upwards; ascending.

asper, -a, -um (as'-per). Rough.

atratus, -a, -um (a-tray'-tus). Blackish; dark.

atropurpureus, -a, -um (a-tro-pur-our'-ee-us). Dark purple.

atrorubens (a-tro-rew'-benz). Deep reddish.

augustus, -a, -um (aw-gus'-tus). Majestic; noble; august.

aurantiacus, -a, -um (aw-ran-tee-ay'-kus). Orange colored.

aureoflavus, -a, -um (aw-ree-o-flay'-vus). Golden yellow.

aureus, -a, -um (aw'-ree-us). Gold colored; golden.

auriculatus, -a, -um (aw-rik-yew-lay'-tus). Furnished with earlike appendages; auriculate.

australis, -e (aw-stray'-lis). Southern.

autumnalis, -e (aw-tum-nay'-lis). Autumn flowering; autumnal.

B

barbatulus, -a, -um (bar-bat'-yew-lus). Somewhat bearded.

barbatus, -a, -um (bar-bay'-tus). Bearded i.e., provided or beset with long weak hairs or terminating in a mass of hairs, usually more or less straight and parallel. The negative expressed by *imberbis.*

basilaris, -e (bay-sil-air'-iss). Pertaining to or at the bottom; basal.

bi or *bis-.* In Latin compounds, signifying "two" or "three."

bicolor (bye'-koll-or). Two-colored.

bictoniensis, -e (bik-toh-nee-en'-sis). Refers to Bicton, the seat of Lord Rolle, near Sidmouth.

bigibbus, -a, -um (bye-jib'-bus). Having two small protuberances.

bipunctatus, -a, -um (by-punk-tay'-tus). Having two dots or spots.

blandus, -a, -um (blan'-dus). Pleasing; charming; tempting; alluring.

brachiatus, -a, -um (brack-ee-ay'-tus). Branched or having arms; in *Brassia* it refers to the very long tails; brachiate.

brachypetalus, -a, -um (brack-ee-pet'-a-lus). Having petals like arms.

bractescens (brak-tess'-enz). Having very large bracts or a strong tendency to the development of bracts.

brevis, -e (brev'-is). Short; abbreviated.

brumalis, -e (broo-may'-lis). Winter-flowering.

brunneus, -a, -um (brunn'-ee-us). Brown; russet.

buccinator (buck'-sin-ay-ter). Trumpeter; shaped like a crooked trumpet or shepherd's horn.

bulbiferus, -a, -um (bul-biff'-er-us). Bulb-bearing.

C

caerulescens (see-roo-less'-enz). Having a tendency to blue; approaching dark blue.

caeruleus, -a, -um (see-rool'-ee-us). Pale indigo blue; dark blue.

caesius, -a, -um (see'-see-us). Bluish-gray.

caespitosus, -a, -um (ses-pi-toh'-sus). Growing in tufts or dense clumps; forming a turf or mat.

calcaratus, -a, -um (kal-kar-ay'-tus). Spurred; having a spur; calcarate.

calcareus, -a, -um (kal-kair'-ee-us). Pertaining to or having a preference for lime; calcareous.

calceolatus, -a, -um (kal-see-oh-lay'-tus). Slipper-shaped; shaped like a shoe; calceolate.

callistus, -a, -um (kal-iss'-tus). Very beautiful.

callosus, -a, -um (kal-oh'-sus). Having a hard protuberance or thickening; thick-skinned; with calluses; callose.

calocheilus, -a, -um (kal-oh-kye'-lus). Having a beautiful lip.

campanulatus, -a, -um (kam-pan-yew-lay'-tus). Bell-shaped; cup-shaped with broad base; campanulate.

candidus, -a, -um (kan'-did-us). Pure, lustrous white; shining or pure white.

canescens (kan-ess'-enz). With off-white or gray hairs; canescent.

canus, -a, -um (kay'-nus). Off-white; gray; ash-colored.

capillaris, -e (kap-ill-air'-iss). Hairlike; resembling a hair; very slender.

capitatus, -a, -um (kap-et-ay'-tus). Shaped like a head; growing on a head or dense cluster; capitate.

cardinalis, -e (kar-din-ay'-liss). Scarlet; cardinal red.

carinatus, -a, -um (ka-ri-nayt'-us). Keeled; having a keel or keels; carinate.

carneus, -a, -um (kar'-nee-us). Flesh-colored; deep pink; carneous.

caudatus, -a, -um (kaw-day'-tus). Furnished with a tail or tails; caudate.

caulescens (kaw-less'-enz). Having a tendency to develop stems; producing a visible leafy stem; caulescent.

cebolleta (seh-boh-lee'-ta). The leaves of the *Oncidium,* so called, resemble those of the chive (*Allium schoenoprasum*), the French name of which is ciboullete.

cepifolius, -a, -um (sep-i-foh'-lee-us). Having leaves resembling those of the onion.

ceraceus, -a, -um (se-ray'-see-us). Like wax; waxy; ceraceous.

cernuus, -a, -um (ser-new'-us). Somewhat pendulous; drooping; nodding.

chimaera (kim-eer'-a). A mythological monster that spouted fire.

chlorochilon (klo-ro-kye'-lon). Green-lipped; having a green lip.

chrysanthus, -a, -um (kris-an'-thus). Golden-flowered.

chrystoxus, -a, -um (kris-o-toks'-us). Golden-arched.

ciliaris, -e (sil-ee-air'-is). Fringed with hairs; ciliate.

cinereus, -a, -um (sin-eer'-ee-us). Ash-colored; light gray.

cinnabarinus, -a, -um (sin-na-bar-eye'-nus). Vermilion-colored; cinnabarred.

cinnamomeus, -a, -um (sin-na-moh'-mee-us). Cinnamon-colored; brown, like cinnamon.

cirratus, -a, -um (si-ray'-tus). Equipped with tendrils or cirri; cirrate.

citrinus, -a, -um (si-trye'-nus). Lemon-colored.

citrosmus, -a, -um (si-troz'-mus). Lemon-scented.

clavatus, -a, -um (klav-ay'-tus). Club-shaped; solid cylindrical, slender at the base and gradually thickening upward; clavate.

coccineus, -a, -um (kok-sin'-ee-us). Bright scarlet.

cochlearis, -e (kok-lee-ay'-ris). Spoon-shaped; shaped like one valve of a clam shell.

coelestis, -e (see-less'-tis). Sky-blue.

coeruleus, -a, -um (see-roo'-lee-us). Dark blue.

coloratus, -a, -um (kol-or-ay'-tus). Colored.

comatus, -a, -um (koh-may'-tus). Furnished with hair; hairy.

compactus, -a, -um (kom-pak'-tus). Compact; dense.

concolor (kon'-kol-or). Of the same color throughout; uniformity of hue in sepals and petals.

conopseus, -a, -um (kon-op'-see-us). Resembling a gnat; canopied.

convallarioides (kon-val-lar-i-oh'-i-deez). Resembling a *Convallaria,* or lily-of-the-valley.

cornu-cervi (kor-new-sir'-vee). Stag's horn; flattened like an antler.

cornutus, -a, -um (kor-new'-tus). Horned, or horn-shaped; cornute.

crenulatus, -a, -um (kren-yew-lay'-tus). Somewhat scalloped; minutely crenate; crenulate.

crepidatus, -a, -um (krep-i-day'-tus). Shaped like an old-fashioned sandal or slipper.

cretaceus, -a, -um (kret-ay'-see-tus). Chalky white; pertaining to chalk.

criniferus, -a, -um (kri-niff'-er-us). Hairy; bearing hairs.

crispus, -a, -um (krisp'-us). Finely waved along the margin; closely curled; crisped.

cristatus, -a, -um (kris-tay'-tus). Crested; bearing a crest; cristate.

cruciatus, -a, um (kroo-si-ay'-tus). Cross-like or cross-shaped; in the form of a cross.

cruentus, -a, -um (kroo-en'-tus). The color of blood, or with blood-colored spots.

crystallinus, -a, -um (kris-tal-lye'-nus). Resembling ice in solidity or translucency; crystalline.

cucullatus, -a, -um (kew-kew-lay'-tus). Hooded or hood-shaped; having the margins curved inward to resemble a hood; cucullate.

cucumerinus, -a, -um (kew-kew-mer-eye'-nus). Resembling a cucumber.

cupreus, -a, -um (kew'-pree-us). Copper-colored; coppery.

curvatus, -a, -um (ker-vay'-tus). Curved.

cyaneus, -a, -um (sy-ay'-ne-us).

cymbiformis, -e (sim-bi-form'-iss). Boat-shaped; convex and keeled.

D

dactyloids (dak-til-oh'-i-deez). Resembling fingers; finger-like.

debilis, -e (deb'-ill-is). Weak; frail; not robust.

decorus, -a, -um (dek-o'-rus). Decorative; becoming; comely.

decumbens (dee-kum'-benz). Reclining but with the growing end upright; decumbent.

deflexus, -a, -um (dee-flex'-us). Bent abruptly downward; deflexed.

delicatus, -a, -um (del-i-kay'-tus). Neat and tender; delicate.

deltoideus, -a, -um (del-toy'-dee-us). Broadly triangular; shaped like the Greek letter delta; deltoid.

dendricolus, -a, -um (den-dri-koh'-lus). Living on trees; epiphytic.

dendroideus, -a, -um (den-droy'-dee-us). Treelike; tree-shaped; dendroid.

densiflorus, -a, -um (den-si-flor'-us). Having the flowers densely clustered; densely flowered.

dentatus, -a, -um (den-tay'-tus). Toothed; furnished with teeth; dentate.

dependens (dee-pend'-enz). Hanging down; dependent.

diaphanus, -a, -um (dye-aff'-an-us). Transparent or translucent; diaphanous.

dichromus, -a, -um (dye-kroh'-mus). Two-colored; of two distinct colors.

difformis, -e (dif-form'-is). Of unusual form in comparison with the normal for the genus.

digitatus, -a, -um (dig-i-tay'-tus). Shaped like an open hand; finger-like; digitate.

dipterus, -a, -um (dip'-ter-us). Two-winged; dipterous.

discolor (dis'-kol-or). Of two different and, usually, distinct colors.

dissectus, -a, -um (dis-sek'-tus). Divided into deep lobes or segments; deeply cut; dissected.

distichus, -a, -um (dis'-tik-us). Arranged in two rows or ranks; distichous.

diurnus, -a, -um (dye-urn'-us). Of the daytime; with flowers open during the day; diurnal.

divergens (dy-verj'-enz). Spreading out widely; divergent.

dolabriformis, -e (do-lab-ri-form'-is). Hatchet-shaped.

dolosus, -a, -um (do-loh'-sus). Deceitful; appearing like some other plant.

domingensis, -e (doh-min-gen'-sis). Native of Santo Domingo (now the Dominican Republic).

dubiosus, -a, -um (doo-bee-oh'-sus). Doubtful; not in conformity to the pattern of the genus; dubious.

dulcis, -a, -um (dull'-sis). Sweet.

E

eburneus, -a, -um (ee-burn'-ee-us). Ivory-like; ivory-white.

echinatus, -a, -um (ek-in-ay'-tus). Furnished with prickles or bristles; spiny; echinate.

ecornutus, -a, -um (ee-kor-new'-tus). Without horns; ecornute.

effusus, -a, -um (ef-few'-sus). Loosely spreading; very diffuse; effuse.

elatus, -a, -um (cl-ay'-tus). Tall, taller than the parts or organs of the plant would lead us to expect, or tall in comparison with its near allies.

elegans (el'-e-ganz). Very choice and attractive; worthy of being chosen; elegant.

ensatus, -a, -um (en-say'-tus). Sword-shaped.

ensifolius, -a, -um (en-si-foh'-li-us). Having sword-shaped leaves.

epi-. A Greek prefix signifying 'on' or 'upon.'

equalis, -e (ee-kway'-lis). Equal.

equestris, -e (ee-kwes'-tris). Knightly, courteous, very handsome; pertaining to a horse, or like the rider of a horse.

erectus, -a, -um (ee-rek'-tus). Upright; erect.

erinaceus, -a, -um (e-rin-ay'-see-us). Resembling a hedgehog; spiny; erinaceous.

erosus, -a, -um (ee-roh'-sus). Jagged, as if gnawed; having a ragged edge; erose.

erubescens (e-roo-bess'-enz). Blushing; growing rosy red.

estriatus, -a, -um (es-tri-ay'-tus). Without stripes.

evectus, -a, -um (e-vek'-tus). Exalted, proud, stately.

exalatus, -a, -um (eks-all-tay'-tus). Very tall; lofty; exalted.

exasperatus, -a, -um (eks-as-per-ay'-tus). Roughened; having a rough surface.

excavatus, -a, -um (esk-kav-ay'-tus). Hollowed out.

excellens (eks-sell'-enz). Excelling; excellent.

excelsus, -a, -um (eks-sell'-sus). Tall.

exiguus, -a, -um (eks-igg'-yew-us). Very little; meager; poor.

eximius, -a, -um (eks-imm'-i-us). Out of the ordinary; distinguished.

F

farinosus, -a, -um (fa-ri-noh'-sus). Covered with meal-like powder; mealy; powdery; farinose.

fasciatus, -a, -um (fa-see-ay'-tus). Bound together; clustered or group into bundles; fasciated.

fastosus, -a, -um (fa-stoh'-sus). Proud.

fenestralis, -e (fen-neh-stray'-lis). Pierced or furnished with window-like openings; fenestrate.

ferrugineus, -a, -um (fer-roo-jin'-ee-us). Rust-colored; rusty; ferrugineous.

ferus, -a, -um (fer'-us). Wild.

festivus, -a, -um (fe-stye'-vus). Beautiful; gay; bright; festive.

filiformis, -e (fil-i-form'-mis). Very long, slender, and flexible.

fimbriatus, -a, -um (fim-bree-ay'-tus). Fringed.

flabellatus, -a, -um (fla-bel-lay'-tus). Fan-shaped; flabellate; flabelliform.

flaccidus, -a, -um (flak'-si-dus). Weak, drooping, usually applied to flower-stems; soft, lax, not rigid.

flagelliformis, -e (fla-jell-i-for'-mis). Whip-firm; long and slender like a lash; flagelliform.

flavescens (fla-veh'-senz). Yellowish; turning yellow; flavescent.

flavidus, -a, -um (flav'-i-dus). Yellow; flavid.

flexuosus, -a, -um (flek-shoo-oh'-sus). Bending alternately in opposite directions.

floridus, -a, -um (floor'-i-dus). Literally flowering and thence flourishing; gay, bright, florid.

foliaceus, -a, -um (fo-li-ay'-see-us). Resembling a leaf in texture and appearance; bearing leaves; foliaceous.

foliosus, -a, -um (fo-li-oh'-sus). Leafy; foliose.

formosanus, -a, -um (for-mo-say'-nus). From the island of Formosa.

formosus, -a, -um (for-moh'-sus). Very beautiful in shape; therefore, strikingly ornamental.

fragrans (fray'-granz). Sweet-scented.

fulvus, -a, -um (full'-vus). Tawny; fulvous.

furcatus, -a, -um (fer-kay'-tus). Forked or two-horned; furcate.

furfuraceus, -a, -um (fer-few-ray'-shus). Scurfy; scaly; furfuraceous.

fuscatus, -a, -um (fus-kay'-tus). Brownish; dark; dusky; fuscous.

fusiformis, -e (few-si-for'-mis). Spindle-shaped. narrowed both ways from a swollen middle; fusiform.

G

galeatus, -a, -um (ga-lee-ay'-tus). Helmet-shaped; galeate.

gelidus, -a, -um (jel'-i-dus). From icy-cold regions.

geminatus, -a, -um (jem-i-nay'-tus). In pairs; twin; geminate.

geniculatus, -a, -um (je-nik-yew-lay'-tus). Bent abruptly, like a knee; geniculate.

gibbosus, -a, -um (gib-boh'-sus). Protuberant or swollen on one side; gibbous.

giganteus, -a, -um (jye-gan-tee'-us). Greatly exceeding its co-geners in size and stature; extremely large; gigantic.

gigas (jye'-gas). A giant, in allusion to size, either of plant or flower.

glabratus, -a, -um (glab-ray'-tus). Nearly glabrous, or becoming glabrous with maturity or age; smooth; glabrate.

gladiatus, -a, -um (glad-i-ay'-tus). Having a sword-shaped foliage; swordlike; gladiate.

glaucophyllus, -a, -um (glaw-ko-fill'-us). Having grayish or bluish-green leaves; having a bloom on the leaves.

glaucus, -a, -um (glaw'-kus). Covered with a bluish-gray, bluish-green, or whitish bloom; glaucous.

globosus, -a, -um (glo-boh'-sus). Nearly spherical; round; globose.

glomeratus, -a, -um (glo-mer-ray'-tus). In dense or compact clusters; glomerate.

gloriosus, -a, -um (glow-ri-oh'-sus). Renowned, illustrious, very beautiful; superb, glorious.

glumaceus, -a, -um (gloo-may'-see-us). Chaffy in texture or resembling the awns of wheat; having blumes; glumaceous.

glutinosus, -a, -um (gloo-tin-oh'-sus). Covered with a sticky exudation; glutinous.

gracilis, -e (gras'-ill-is). Slender and thence graceful.

grandis, -e (grand'-is). Big, great, showy, imposing; grand.

gratissimus, -a, -um (grat-iss'-i-mus). Very agreeable; pleasing.

graveolens (grav-ee-oh'-lenz). Strong smelling; heavy scented; rank.

grossus, -a, -um (groh'-sus). Very large.

guatemalensis, -e (gwat-i-ma-len'-sis). A native of Guatemala.

guttatus, -a, -um (gut-tay'-tus). Spotted; speckled with small dots; guttate.

H

harpophyllus, -a, -um (har-po-fill'-us). Having sickle-shaped leaves.

hastatus, -a, -um (has-tay'-tus). Like an arrowhead; spear-shaped; hastate.

hastilabius, -a, -um (has-ti-lay'-bee-us). With a spear-shaped lip.

hirsutissimus, -a, -um (her-soo-tiss'-ee-muss). Very hairy; most hairy.

hispidus, -a, -um (hiss'-pid-us). Beset with rigid or bristly hairs or with bristles; hispid.

humilis, -e (hew'-mil-is). Low-growing; more dwarf than most of its kind.

hyacinthinus, -a, -um (hye-a-sin-thye'-nus). Resembling a hyacinth.

hyphaematicus, -a, -um (hye-fee-mat'-i-kus). Blood red underneath.

I

igneus, -a, -um (ig'-nee-us). Fiery color, red; igneous.

illustris, -e (ill-lus'-tris). Brilliant; lustrous.

imbricatus, -a, -um (im-bree-kay'-tus). Overlapping, like shingles on a roof, either vertically or spirally; imbricate.

incanus, -a, -um (in-kay'-nus). Hoary; quite gray; incanescent; canescent.

incarnatus, -a, -um (in-kar-nay'-tus). Flesh-colored.

incisus, -a, -um (in-sye'-sus). Deeply and irregularly cut; incised.

incurvus, -a, -um (in-ker'-vus). Crooked, bent; curved inward.

induratus, -a, -um (in-dew-ray'-tus). Hard, hardened.

infundibuliformis, -e (in-fund-dib-yew-li-form'-is). Funnel-form, trumpet-shaped; infundibuliform.

inscriptus, -a, -um (in-skrip'-tus). Marked, as if with letters; inscribed.

intermedius, -a, -um (in-ter-mee'-di-us). Halfway between two other things; intermediate in color, form or habit.

interruptus, -a, -um (in-ter-rupp'-tus). Not continuous, as with scattered leaves or flowers; interrupted.

iridifolius, -a, -um (eye-rid-i-foh'-li-us). Iris-leaved.

irroratus, -a, -um (ir-roy-ay'-tus). Dewy; moistened, sprinkled with dew; irrorate.

J

japonicus, -a, -um (ja-pon'-ik-us). Native of Japan; Japanese.

javanicus, -a, -um (ja-van'-ik-us). Native of Java; Javanese.

juncifolius, -a, -um (jun-si-foh'-lee-us). Rush-leaved.

L

labiatus, -a, -um (lab-i-ay'-tus). Large-lipped; having a lip; labiate.

labyrinthiformis, -e (lab-i-rin-thee-form'-iss). With intricate winding lines or passages; labyrinthine.

laceratus, -a, -um (la-ser-ray'-tus). Torn; irregularly cleft or cut; lacerate.

lacinatus, -a, -um (la-sin-i-ay'-tus). Slashed; cut into narrow pointed segments; laciniate.

lacunosus, -a, -um (lak-yew-no'-sus). Having holes or empty places; deeply pitted lacunose.

laevigatus, -a, -um (lee-vig-ay'-tus). Having a smooth, polished surface.

lanceolatus, -a, -um (lan-see-o-lay'-tus). Shaped like the head of a lance; spear-shaped; narrow and tapering toward the apex or toward each end; lanceolate.

lanuginosus, -a, -um (lan-oo-jin-oh'-sus). Woolly or cottony; covered with soft downy hairs; lanuginose.

latifolius, -a, -um (lat-i-foh'-lee-us). Broad-leaved.

latilabrus, -a, -um (lat-i-lay'-brus). Broad-lipped.

laxus, -a, -um (laks'-us). Loose, or open; lax.

lentiginosus, -a, -um (len-tij-in-oh'-sus). Freckled; lentiginose.

leonis (lee-oh'-niss). Of a lion, in the sense of strong, stout, leonine.

leopardinus, -a, -um (lee-o-par-dye'-nus). Tawny, or conspicuously spotted like a leopard.

lepidotus, -a, -um (le-pi-doh'-tus). Covered with small scurfy scales; lepidote.

lepidus, -a, -um (lep'-id-us). Neat, pretty, pleasing; graceful; elegant.

leptosepalus, -a, -um (lep-to-sep'-al-us). Having slender sepals.

leucorrhodus, -a, -um (lew-ko-roh'-dus). Rosy-white.

lilacinus, -a, -um (lye-la-sye'-nus). Like lilac in color or form.

limbatus, -a, -um (lim-bay'-tus). Having a distinct border of some other color; limbate.

linguiformis, -e (ling-gwee-for'-miss). Tongue-shaped; linguiform.

lividus, -a, -um (liv'-id-us). Lead colored; bluish-gray; livid.

longicornu (lon-jee-kor'-noo). Having a long horn.

longifolius, -a, -um (lon-jee-foh'-lee-us). Long-leaved.

loratus, -a, -um (lor-ay'-tus). Strap-shaped; lorate.

lunatus, -a, -um (loo-nay'-tus). Crescent-shaped; lunate.

luridus, -a, -um (lew'-rid-us). Dismal-colored; yellowish brown; lurid.

luteolus, -a, -um (loo-tee-oh'-lus). Pale yellow; yellowish.

luteo-purpureus, -a, -um (loo'-tee-o-poor-poor'-e-us). Yellowish purple or yellow and purple.

luteus, -a, -um (lew'-tee-us). Golden-yellow; luteous.

lutescens (loo-tess'-sens). Yellowish; becoming yellow; lutescent.

M

macranthus, -a, -um (ma-kran'-thus). Large-flowered.

macrochilus, -a, -um (mak-ro-kye'-lus). Large-lipped.

maculatus, -a, -um (mak-yew-lay'-tus). Spotted; maculate.

maculosus, -a, -um (mak-yew-loh'-sus). Spotted; maculate.

magnificus, -a, -um (mag-nif'-ik-us). Showy; magnificent.

magnus, -a, -um (mag'-nus). Great; large; big.

majalis, -e (ma-jay'-lis). Flowering in May.

major (may'-jor). Larger than its cogeners.

majus, -a, -um (may'-jus). Large compared with others of the same genus.

marginalis, -e (mar-jin-ay'-lis). Placed upon or attached to the edge.

maxillaris, -e (mak-sil-lair'-iss). Resembling jaws.

maximus, -a, -um (mak'-sim-us). The largest of its kind; maximal.

medusae (me-dew'-see). Referring to Medusa, one of the Gorgons whose locks Minerva changed into serpents.

meleagris, -e (mel-ee-ay'-gris). Resembling or spotted like a Guinea hen.

membranaceus, -a, -um (mem-bran-ay'-shus). Thin and semi-transparent; shinlike; membranaceous.

microchilus, -a, -um (mye-kro-kye'-lus). Small-lipped.

militaris, -e (mil-it-ay'-ris). Pertaining to soldiers, like a soldier.

miniatus, -a, -um (min-ee-ay'-tus). Vermilion-colored; cinnabar-red; miniaceous.

minimus, -a, -um (min'-i-mus). Smallest; minimum.

minus, -a, -um (mye'-nus). Smaller.

minutus, -a, -um (mye-new'-tus). Very small; minute.

minutissimus, -a, -um (mye-new-tiss'-i-mus). The very smallest; most minute.

mirabilis, -e (mye-rab'-il-is). Wonderful; remarkable; marvelous.

mitriformis, -e (mye-tri-for'-miss). Mitre-shaped, or like a cap.

moniliformis, -e (mo-nil-i-for'-miss). Necklace-like; having alternate swellings and constrictions.

moscifera (ma-skiff'-er-a). Bearing flies; alluding to the resemblance of some flowers to a fly.

moschatus, -a, -um (mos-kay'-tus). Musk-scented.

multiflorus, -a, -um (mul-tee-flor'-us). Many-flowered.

muralis, -e (mew-ray'-lis). Growing on walls.

mutabilis, -e (mew-tab'-il-is). Changeable, especially as to color.

myrianthus, -a, -um (meer-ee-an'-thus). Innumerable-flowered.

N

nanellus, -a -um (nan-ell'-us). Very dwarf.

nanus, -a, -um (nay'-nus). Dwarf.

natans (nay'-tanz). Floating.

navicularis, -e (nav-ik-yew-lay'-ris). Boat-shaped; cymbiform; navicular.

nemoralis, -e (nem-o-ray'-lis). Growing in groves or shady places; nemoral.

niger, nigra, nigrum (nye'-jer). Black.

nigrescens (nye-gress'-enz). Blackish; nigrescent.

nitidus, -a, -um (nit'-id-us). Shining; nitidous.

nitens (nye'-tenz). Shining; becoming shiny.

nivalis, -e (niv-ay'-lis). Snowy white; nival.

nobilis, -e (noh'-bil-is). Eminent; remarkable for fine qualities; noble.

nocturnus, -a, -um (nok-tern'-us). Night-flowering; blooming at night.

notatus, -a, -um (no-tay'-tus). Spotted; marked.

nubigenus, -a, -um (new-bi-jen'-us). Born among the clouds; from a high elevation.

nudus, -a, -um (new'-dus). Naked; bare; nude.

nutans (new'-tanz). Nodding; nutant.

O

obryzatus, -a, -um (o-bry-zay'-tus). Pure gold color.

obtusus, -a, -um (ob-too'-sus). Blunt or rounded at the tip.

ochraceus, -a, -um (o-kray'-see-us). Yellowish; ochre-colored; ochraceous.

oculatus, -a, -um (ok-hew-lay'-tus). Having one or more dark spots like eyes; oculate.

odontochilus, -a, -um (o-don-toh-kye'-lus). Having a toothed lip.

odoratus, -a, -um (o-do-ray'-tus). Fragrant.

odoratissimus, -a, -um (o-do-ra-tiss'-i-mus). Very fragrant.

oncidioides (on-sid-di-oy'-deez). Resembling an *Oncidium.*

ornithorhynchus, -a, -um (or-nith-o-rink'-us). Resembling the beak of a bird.

ovalis, -e (o-vay'-liss). Broadly elliptic in shape; oval.

P

pallens (pal'-lenz). Becoming pale or light in color.

pallidus, -a, -um (pal'-li-dus). Pale, pallid.

palmatus, -a, -um (pal-may'-tus). Lobed and radiating like the fingers; palmate.

panduratus, -a, -um (pan-dew-ray'-tus). Shaped like a violin; pandurate.

paniculatus, -a, -um (pan-ik-yew-lay'-tus). With flowers arranged in panicles; paniculate.

papilio (pa-pill'-ee-o). A butterfly.

pardinus, -a, -um (par-dye'-nus). Spotted like a leopard or panther.

peduncularis, -e (pee-dunk-yew-lay'-riss). Having long peduncles or peduncular flower-stalks.

pendulus, -a, -um (pen'-dew-luss). Hanging or drooping; pendulous.

perbellus, -a, -um (per-bell'-us). Very beautiful.

peruvianus, -a, -um (per-roo'-vee-an-us). Peruvian; from Peru.

petiolatus, -a, -um (pet-i-o-lay'-tus). Having a petiole; petiolate.

phoenicius, -a, -um (fee-nish'-us). Purple-red.

phymatochilus, -a, -um (fye-mat-o-kye'-lus). Having a swelling on the lip.

picturatus, -a, -um (pik-tew-ray'-tus). Variegated.

pictus, -a, -um (pik'-tus). Painted.

pileatus, -a, -um (pil-ee-ay'-tus). Furnished with a cap.

pinnatus, -a, -um (pin-nay'-tus). Feather-like, having leaflets arranged on each side of a common stalk; pinnate.

placatus, -a, -um (plak-ay'-tus). Quiet; calm; placid.

planus, -a, -um (play'-nus). Flat; plane.

plenus, -a, -um (plee'-nus). Double or full.

plicatus, -a, -um (plye-kay'-tus). Folded like a fan, or pleated; plicate.

plumosus, -a, -um (ploo-moh'-sus). Feathery; feather-like; plumose.

polyanthus, -a, -um (pol-i-an'-thus). Many-flowered.

polybulbon (pol-i-bul'-bon). Having many bulbs.

praecox (pree'-koks). Early blooming; very early; precocious.

praestans (pree'-stanz). Standing in front; excelling; distinguished.

prasinus, -a, -um (pray-sye'-nus). Grass-green.

primulinus, -a, -um (prim-yew-lye'-nus). Resembling a primrose.

princeps (prin'-seps). Distinguished.

prismatocarpus, -a, -um (priz-mat-o-kar'-pus). Having prism-shaped seed-pods, with three flat sides and three sharp angles.

proboscideus, -a, -um (proh-bos-sid'-ee-us). Snoutlike.

procumbens (pro-kum'-benz). Prostrate; lying flat along the ground.

profusus, -a, -um (proh-few'-sus). Abundant; profuse.

pruinosus, -a, -um (prew-in-oh'-sus). Covered with a whitish, frost-like bloom; excessively glaucous; pruinose.

pubescens (pew-bess'-enz). Downy; covered with fine short hair; pubescent.

pudicus, -a, -um (pew'-dik-us). Modest; bashful.

pulchellus, -a, -um (pul-kel'-lus). Fair, pretty.

pulcher, pulchra, pulchrum (pul'-ker). Beautiful, lovely.

pullus, -a, -um (pull'-us). Dark-colored.

pulvinatus, -a, -um (pull-vin-ay'-tus). Formed like or resembling a cushion.

pumilus, -a, -um (pew'-mill-us). Dwarf, or low-growing.

punctatus, -a, -um (punk-tay'-tus). Spotted; marked with dots, depressions or translucent glands; punctate.

purpurascens (per-per-ras'-senz). Becoming or turning purple.

purpuratus, -a, -um (per-per-ay'-tus). Marked with purple so as to have a certain regal quality.

purpureus, -a, -um (per-per'-ee-us). Purple.

purus, -a, -um (poor'-us). Spotless; of one color.

pusillus, -a, -um (pew-sill'-us). Very small.

pygmaeus, -a, -um (pig-mee'-us). Pygmy; very small.

pyramidalis, -e (peer-a-mid-day'-liss). Pyramid-shaped; pyramidal.

pyriformis, -e (peer-i-for'-miss). Pear-shaped; pyriform.

Q

quadratus, -a, -um (kwad-ray'-tus). Four-sided.

quadricolor (kwad'-ri-ko-lor). Four-colored.

quadricornis, -e (kwad-ri-kor'-niss). Four-horned.

quinatus, -a, -um (kwin-ay'-tus). In fives.

quinquenervis, -e (kwin-kwe-ner'-viss). Having five nerves or veins.

quinquevulnerus, -a, -um (kwin-kwe-vul'-ner-us). Having five wounds, or blood-red spots.

R

racemosus, -a, -um (ras-see-moh'-sus). With flowers borne in racemes, resembling a raceme; racemose.

radiatus, -a, -um (ray-di-ay'-tus). Spreading out from a common center; with rays; radiate.

radicans (rad'-ik-anz). Having rooting stems.

ramosus, -a, -um (ram-oh'-sus). Branched; ramose.

raniferus, -a, -um (ran-nif'-fer-us). Bearing frogs.

rarus, -a, -um (rare'-us). Rare; uncommon.

recurvus, -a, -um (ree-ker'-vus). Bent backward, recurved.

reflexus, -a, -um (ree-flek'-sus). Abruptly bent backward or downward; reflexed.

refulgens (ree-ful'-jenz). Shining brightly.

regalis, -e (ree-gay'-liss). Of outstanding merit; regal.

reginae (rej-hye'-nee). Of the queen; queenly.

regius, -a, -um (ree'-ji-us). Royal; regal.

reniformis, -e (ree-ni-for'-miss). Kidney-shaped; reniform.

repens (ree'-penz). Creeping; prostrate and rooting at the nodes; repent.

reticulatus, -a, -um (re-tik-yew-lay'-tus). In the form of a network; reticulate.

roseus, -a, -um (roh'-zee-us). Rose-colored; delicate pink; rosy.

rostratus, -a, -um (ros-tray'-tus). Having a projection like the beak of a bird; beaked; rostrate.

rotundatus, -a, -um (ro-tun-day'-tus). Nearly circular; rounded; rotund.

rubellus, -a, -um (roo-bel'-us). Reddish-colored.

ruber, rubra, rubrum (roo'-ber). Red. In compound words, *rubri-.*

rubescens (roo-bess'-senz). Rosy red, or suffused with rose; blushing; reddish-colored.

rubro-oculatus, -a, -um (roo-bro-ok-yew-lay'-tus). Red-eyed.

rubro-purpureus, -a, -um (roo-broo-poor-poor'-ee-us). Reddish purple.

rubiginosus, -a, -um (roo-bij-in-oh'-sus). Rusty; rust-colored; rubiginous.

rufescens (roo-fess'-senz). Reddish brown.

rugosus, -a, -um (roo-goh'-sus). Roughened by wrinkles; rugose.

rugulosus, -a, -um (roo-gew-low'-sus). Minutely rugose; finely wrinkled; rugulose.

rupestris, -e (roo-pess'-triss). Growing in rocky places; rock-loving.

rupicolus, -a, -um (roo-pik'-o-lus). Growing in cliffs and ledges; rupicolous.

S

saccatus, -a, -um (sak-kay'-tus). Pouch- or bag-shaped; saccate.

sagittatus, -a, -um (saj-it-tay'-tus). Shaped like an arrowhead, with the basal lobes directed downward.

sanguineus, -a, -um (sang-gwin'-e-us). Blood-colored; blood-red; sanguine.

sanguinolentus, -a, -um (sang-gwin-o-len'-tus). Having blood-red spots or veins.

sapidus, -a, -um (sap'-id-us). Pleasant to taste; sapid.

sarcodes (sar-koh'-deez). Of flesh-like substance.

saxicolus, -a, -um (sax'-ik-o-lus). Growing on rocks; saxicolous.

scandens (skan'-denz). Climbing; scandent.

sculptus, -a, -um (skulp'-tus). Carved; sculpted.

scutellaris, -e (skew-tell-ay'-ris). Dish- or shield-shaped.

scuticaria (skoo-ti-kar'-ee-a). A very small genus of three species of epiphytic orchids from South America, related to *Maxillaria,* it was established by Lindley in 1843, the name referring to the whip-like character of the pendent, terete leaves.

secundus, -a, -um (sek-kun'-dus). One-sided; borne along one side of an axis; secund.

selligerus, -a, -um (sel-lij'-er-us). Saddle-shaped.

senilis, -e (sen-nye'-liss). Like an old man; white-haired; senile.

sericeus, -a, -um (ser-iss'-e-us). Silky; covered with silky down; sericeous.

serpens (ser'-penz). Creeping.

serratus, -a, -um (ser-ay'-tus). Having sharp teeth pointing forward; serrate.

sesquipedalis, -e (sess-kwee-pee-day'-liss). One-and-a-half feet long.

setaceus, -a, -um (se-tay'-see-us). Bristle-like or bristle-shaped; furnished with bristles; setaceous.

siliceus, -a, -um (si-liss'-e-us). Growing in sand; siliceous.

silvestris, -e (sil-ves'-triss). Growing in woods.

sinensis, -e (si-nen'-sis). Chinese, or from China.

solaris, -e (so-lay'-ris). Growing in sunny places.

sordidus, -a, -um (sor'-did-us). Dirty; usually meaning dull-colored; sordid.

speciosissimus, -a, -um (spee-see-o-siss'-i-mus). Eminently handsome, uniting elegance of form and brilliancy of color.

speciosus, -a, -um (spee-see-oh'-sus). Handsome in form and color; showy; fair.

spectabilis, -e (spek-tab'-il-is). Deserving especial notice by reason of intrinsic worth; spectacular.

sphacelatus, -a -um (sfass-ee-lay'-tus). Scorched; dead; diseased; some part looking as if withered; sphacelate.

splendens (splen'-denz). Showy and handsome; radiant or shining; lustrous; splendid.

squalens (skway'-lenz). Dirty; becoming dull in color.

squalidus, -a, -um (skway'-li-dus). Dirty; usually applied to flowers of dull color.

stapelioides (sta-pee-lee-oy'-deez). Resembling a *Stapelia.*

stellatus, -a, -um (stell-ay'-tus). Star-shaped; resembling a star; stellate.

stramineus, -a, -um (stra-min'-e-us). Strawlike or straw-colored; stramineous.

streptopetalus, -a, -um (strep-toh-pet'-alus). With twisted petals.

striatus, -a, -um (stry-ay'-tus). Striped; marked with longitudinal lines, grooves, or ridges; striate.

strictus, -a, -um (strik'-tus). Very straight and upright; erect.

suaveolens (swav-e-oh'-lenz). Sweet-smelling.

suavis, -e (sway'-viss). Sweet-scented; agreeable; delightful.

suavissimus, -a, -um (swav-iss'-i-mus). Very fragrant.

sulphureus, -a, -um (sull-few'-re-us). Sulphur-colored, light-yellow.

sumatranus, -a, -um (soo-may-tray'-nus). Native of Sumatra.

superbiens (sue-per'-bi-enz). Becoming grand and stately.

superbus, -a, -um (sue-per'-bus). Excellent, splendid; superb.

sylvaticus, -a, -um (sill-vat'-i-kus). Of the woodlands or forests.

sylvestris, -e (sill-vest'-ris). Growing in woods; forest-loving.

T

tenebrosus, -a, -um (ten-eh-broh'-sus). Dark; growing in shaded places.

tenuifolius, -a, -um (ten-yew-i-foh'-li-us). Slender-leaved.

teres (teh'-reez). Long and cylindrical; terete.

teretifolius, -a, -um (teh-ree-ti-foh'-li-us). Having terete leaves.

terrestris, -e (ter-rest'-tris). Of the ground; growing in the ground or opposed to growing in trees or in water.

tessellatus, -a, -um (tess-sel-lay'-tus). Arranged in a checkered or mosaic pattern; tessellated.

thyrsiflorus, -a, -um (thur-si-flor'-us). Having flowers in a thyrse or compact, clustered panicle.

tibinis, -e (tib-i-sye'-niss). Of a flute-player; resembling a flute or trumpet.

tigrinus, -a, -um (ti-grye'-nus). Striped or spotted like a tiger.

titanus, -a, -um (ty-tay'-nus). Very large; titanic.

tomentosus, -a, -um (to-men-toh'-sus). Densely pubescent with matted hairs; woolly; tomentose.

tortilis, -e (tor'-ti-liss). Twisted; coiled; tortile.

tricolor (trye'-col-or). Three-colored.

tripudians (trye-pew'-di-anz). Dancing.

tripunctatus, -a, -um (trye-punk-tay'-tus). Three-spotted.

triquetrus, -a, -um (trye-kwee'-trus). Three-cornered.

tristie, -e (tris'-tiss). Dull-colored; dull; sad.

triumphans (trye-um'-fanz). Conquering; excelling all others; triumphant.

tropicus, -a, -um (trop'-ik-us). Of or from the tropics.

tubatus, -a, -um (tew-bay'-tus). Trumpet-shaped.

tuberculatus, -a, -um (tew-ber-kew-lay'-tus). Covered with wart-like excrescences; tuberculate.

tuberosus, -a, -um (tew-ber-oh'-sus). Having the character of a tuber; tuberlike in appearance; tuberous.

typicus, -a, -um (tip'-ik-us). Agreeing with the type of a group; typical.

U

umbrosus, -a, -um (um-broh'-sus). In or like an umbel; umbellate.

undulatus, -a, -um (un-dew-lay'-tus). Waved; wavy; with a wavy margin or surface; undulate.

unguiculatus, -a, -um (un-gwik-yew-lay'-tus). Contracted at the base into a claw or narrow stalk; unguiculate.

unicornis, -e (yew-ni-kor'-niss). One-horned.

uniflorus, -a, -um (yew-ni-flor'-us). One-flowered, or having single-flowered peduncles.

urceolatus, -a, -um (er-see-o-lay'-tus). Hollow and cylindrical or ovoid, and contracted at or below the mouth like an urn; urn-shaped; urceolate.

utricularioides (yew-trik-yew-la-ri-oy'-deez). Resembling the Bladderwort, *Utricularia*.

V

vagans (vay'-ganz). Of wide distribution; wandering.

variabilis, -e (va-ri-ay'-bil-liss). Varying in form or color; variable.

variegatus, -a, -um (vair-ri-gay'-tus). Irregularly colored in patches; blotched; variegated.

velatus, -a, -um (vel-lay'-tus). Veiled.

velutinus, -a, -um (vel-yew'-tin-us). Velvety; soft; velutinous.

venosus, -a, -um (vee-noh'-sus). Veined; having many or prominent veins; venous; venose.

venustus, -a, -um (vee-nus'-tus). Comely; graceful; ladylike; charming.

verecundus, -a, -um (veh-re-kun'-dus). Modest, shy, coy; blushing; verecund.

vernalis, -e (ver-nay'-liss). Of the spring; spring-flowering; vernal.

verrucosus, -a, -um (ver-rew-koh'-sus). Covered with wartlike elevations or excrescences; verrucose.

versicolor (ver'-si-kul-er). Changeable in color; variously colored; versicolor.

verticillatus, -a, -um (ver-tis-sil-lay'-tus). Arranged in a whorl, like the spokes of a wheel.

vespertinus, -a, -um (ves-per-tye'-nus). Of the evening; evening-blooming.

vestalis, -e (ves-tay'-liss). Virginlike; chaste; vestal.

villosus, -a, -um (vill-oh'-sus). Shaggy; clothed with long, soft hairs; villous; villose.

violaceus, -a, -um (vye-o-lay'-see-us). Violet-colored; violaceous.

violescens (vye-o-less'-enz). Almost violet-colored; turning violet.

virens (vye'-renz). Fresh-looking; lively green.

virescens (vih-reh'-senz). Light green; having a tendency to turn green.

virgatus, -a -um (ver-gay'-tus). Rod-like; long, slender, and straight; twiggy; virgate.

virginalis, -e (ver-jin-ay'-liss). Maidenly; pure white; virginal.

viridescens (vir-i-dess'-enz). Becoming green.

viridipurpureus, -a, -um (vi'-rid-i-poor-poor'-e-us). Greenish purple.

viridiflorus, -a, -um (vi-rid-i-flor'-us). With green flowers; green-flowered.

viridis, -e (vir'-i-diss). Green.

vitellinus, -a, -um (vye-tell-lye'-nus). The color of an egg yolk; vitelline.

volutus, -a, -um (vo-loo'-tus). Rolled up like a scroll; having rolled leaves; volute.

volubilis, -e (vol-yew'-bil-iss). Twining; rolling; turning.

vulgaris, -e (vul-gay'-riss). Common; ordinary.

X

xanthinus, -a, -um (zan-thye'-nus). Yellow; yellowish; xanthous.
xanthodon (zan'-thoh-dun). Yellow-toothed.
xantholeucus, -a, -um (zan-tho-lew'-kuss). Yellowish white.
xiphifolius, -a, -um (ziff-i-foh'-li-us). Iris-leaved; swordlike.

Y

ybaguensis, -e (also *ibaguensis, -e*) (ee-ba-gwen'-siss). Native of Ybague or Ibague, Colombia.

Z

zebrinus, -a, -um (ze-brye'-nus). Zebra striped; striped.
zonatus, -a, -um (zoh-nay'-tus). Banded or marked with a zone of a distinct color; zonate.

List of Color Illustrations